IN THE
KITCHEN
WITH GOD

Quiet Moments with God

RACINE, WI

In the Kitchen with God
ISBN: 978-1-970103-90-8 - *Paperback*
ISBN: 978-1-970103-91-5 - *Hardcover*
ISBN: 978-1-970103-53-3 - *Ebook*

Copyright © 2022 by Honor Books
Racine, WI

Cover Design by Faille Schmitz

Contributing writers: Nancy B. Gibbs, Sarah M. Hupp, Elsa Lynch, Barbara Scott, Conover Swofford, and Nanette Thorsen-Snipes.

Sit Back and Relax

I remember the days of long ago; I meditate on all your works and consider what your hands have done.

P S A L M   1 4 3 : 5

Scientists and psychologists tell us that odors have a profound impact on memory. Their extensive research indicates that when presented with certain smells, people remember long-dormant events in their lives.

We could have saved them a lot of time and money! Most of us don't have to be told how powerful the sense of smell is. Who among us has not been startled by a sudden memory stirred up by the aroma of baking bread? We're taken back to our childhood simply by a whiff of roast beef or chicken soup simmering on the stove top.

Have you ever noticed how kitchens retain a certain odor even when there's nothing cooking at the moment? In the same way, many kitchens retain the personality of the cook of the house. In most families, the cook is a woman, and we naturally associate the aroma of food with our mothers and our grandmothers.

A kitchen is so much more than a place to prepare food. It's the hub of family activity, a place of fellowship—and often, a place of solitude. It's also a place where we can meet God, through the act of saying grace or silently talking with Him as we make dinner and wash the dishes or reading His Word with our morning coffee or our midnight snack.

Then, as always, "We are to God the aroma of Christ" (2 Corinthians 2:15).

When you feel as though you're stuck in the kitchen, just remember—you're *In the Kitchen with God.* That should change your entire outlook!

Rise and Shine

Take my yoke upon you and learn from me, for I am gentle and humble in heart, and you will find rest for your souls.
MATTHEW 11:29

———————————————

J anie jolted awake at the sound of her alarm clock. This was her third day waking up in the middle of the night . . . at least it felt like the middle of the night even though it was actually early morning. She was not at all sure why she went through the trouble. It especially seemed vague and worthless the moments before her head settled back down onto the pillow.

"No!" She yelled at herself, waking up again with a start. She had promised she would do this and she was going to, even if she went around for the rest of the day with a sleep-deprived, grumpy attitude. Janie stumbled to the bathroom, splashed some water on her face and carefully traversed the steps. Downstairs, she started a pot of coffee and sat down at the kitchen table. She had originally started doing her devotions on the sofa, only to discover they only lasted the five minutes it took for her to fall asleep again. At the kitchen table, she took out her Bible, her notebook, and a devotional. Her attitude brightened.

Once she was up, every moment was worth it. Meeting God in the early morning hours didn't make her grumpy as she always anticipated, but instead they revitalized her and brought her peace. The early morning moments gave her a chance to see the sunrise, to watch an occasional bird, to enjoy the silence of a world not yet awake. It took a while to convince her body of the benefits of such early rising, but soon it became habit. After a while, the only time she experienced grumpiness was when she missed her morning meeting with God.

Gods yoke is light; He is the rest for our souls that we think sleep should bring. Taking the time with our Savior in the early morning hours is better than fine cappuccino, the smell of omelets, and bacon. It is the best part of our day.

_____

Faulty but Familiar

*In all the travels of the Israelites, whenever the
cloud lifted from above the tabernacle, they
would set out.*
EXODUS 40:36

———————————————————

T he Israelites had this cloud, Mom," Ellie's
six-year-old exclaimed as the children
tumbled into the car after Sunday school. "It
was bigger than a thunderhead."

"Yeah, and at night it had fire in it brighter than a
street light, so no one had to be afraid of the dark,"
echoed Ellie's timid four-year-old as she recalled the
details of the Bible story they had heard.

"Every time the cloud moved, the people had to
move," the six-year-old continued. "That would be
great. You wouldn't be stuck in the same campground
for forty years!"

Their spirited chattering continued on the short
drive home as they shared that the Israelites never

knew how long they would be in one campsite. Whenever Gods cloud began to move, the Israelites were required to pack up and move, too.

Moving would mean tearing your household apart. Every housewife in Israel would have to quickly dry the dishes, tear down her kitchen, repack the pots and pans, load everything onto the donkey cart, and follow after God's cloud. Then, when the cloud stopped, everything would have to be unloaded, unpacked, and re-set.

As Ellie walked into her kitchen that day, she took a close look at the linoleum that was gouged in places and the cupboards in need of another coat of paint. The contents of the overfilled trash can formed a precarious pyramid. The faucet still dripped annoyingly, and the dishes from breakfast sat piled on the counter. Yet with all its faults and peculiarities, it was home.

As her family bustled off to other parts of the house, Ellie sat down quietly at the kitchen table. "Thank You God for my kitchen," she said out loud. "I don't care if it does have drips and gouges and flaws. At least it's a kitchen that stays in one place!"

Apple Pie Problems

He who was seated on the throne said,
"I am making everything new!"
REVELATION 21:5

———————————————

Peel. Core. Season. Mix. The steps for making Marilyns favorite apple pie rolled from her fingertips without a pause. The piecrust lay trimmed and ready in the pie pan, awaiting the seasoned filling.

Everything looked just fine. Yet as she added a sprinkling of walnuts and placed the top crust in position, a heavy sigh escaped from her lips.

It was probably a good thing that this was a familiar recipe. Marilyn's mind was not on the pie but rather on a troubled relationship with a close friend. No matter how she tried to solve the problem, things only seemed to grow worse. What do I do now? she wondered.

As she slid the pie into the oven, Marilyn remembered a speaker at a seminar who encouraged her listeners to keep a prayer journal. The speaker said she usually prayed aloud as she wrote her concerns in a journal, and that simple exercise clarified her problems and helped her keep track of Gods answers.

Marilyn picked up a blank book she had been given for Christmas. Sitting at the kitchen table, she began to write a letter to God, pouring out her heart and her hurt about this troubled relationship. Before she knew it, the oven timer sounded, and she sniffed the familiar warm scent of apples filling the room. She closed the cover on several pages of scrawled script.

Surprisingly, her heart felt lighter. She was struck by the similarity between the pie and the prayer journal. Wrapped between two pie crusts and left to time and the work of the oven, the apples were still apples, but their taste and texture had changed from tart and crisp to sweet and smooth. In the same way, Marilyn had wrapped her concerns between the covers of prayer. As she set the pie on top of the stove, God reassured her that all she needed was to give Him time to work. He would change that soured relationship and make things sweet again.

Scheduled Rest

[Jesus] said to them, "Come with me by
yourselves to a quiet place and get some rest."
MARK 6:31

S chedules. Sometimes we feel as though we're governed by to-do lists. The kitchen calendar overflows with notations: do this, go here, pick that up, buy this, deliver that, or mail this other thing. And just when we think we're on top of our lives, someone adds a new item to our to-do list.

Researchers say that Americans today are plagued with more stress-related health problems than any other generation in history. Stress is a contributing factor to heart disease and high blood pressure and has been linked to an increase in bad cholesterol and the worsening of arthritis.

How can we keep the daily pressures of life from becoming debilitating stress? God's solution has always been to take a day of rest. Return to the simple pleasures of the kitchen. The kitchen in our great-grandmothers' time was both the center of family activity and the center of rest. Family meals were made and shared around a common table. Conversation was the primary form of entertainment—not the television, radio, or compact disc player with headphones. Comforting aromas greeted family members throughout the day. And nothing could beat the smell of a chicken roasting in the oven for Sunday dinner.

So toss out the bottle of aspirin and put your daily planner away for one day each week. Make sure everyone in the family knows that this will be a "scheduled" day of rest. Before you go to bed the night before, use your modern appliances to help give you a jump-start on the day. Pop some dough ingredients in the bread machine and set the timer on the coffeepot. You'll awaken to the smell of freshly perked coffee and freshly baked bread. Those inviting aromas will make you want to linger in the kitchen—to chat, to laugh, to love, and to rest. God—and our great-grandmothers—will be pleased.

Penny from Heaven

Some trust in chariots and some in horses,
but we trust in the name of the Lord our God.
PSALM 20:7

Kevin brushed the sandy-colored hair from his eyes. "Mom, I have a chance to be president of the fourth grade!" He reached for a cinnamon roll and poured some milk into a glass.

"You know, son, that it'll be a tough race."

The boy took a swallow of milk and wiped his face with his sleeve. "I know, Mom. But I just know I can do it."

His mother reached into the pocket of her jeans and pulled out a penny. "I tell you what, why don't you take my penny from heaven to keep your spirits up?"

The boy grinned and put the penny in his pocket. He gathered his books and stuck them haphazardly into his book bag, then slung the bag over his shoulder.

Adrienne busied herself with everyday chores, wondering if her little boy would come home disappointed by failure or elated by victory. When 3:15 finally arrived, she was ready with his favorite chocolate chip cookies.

Kevin banged in the back door, his face beaming. He tugged on his baseball cap and cocked his head to one side. "I did it, Mom!" he said. "I'm the new president of the fourth-grade class!"

Kevin caught his breath and settled down in front of his plate of cookies.

With his mouth full, he said, "I can't believe it, Mom! I just can't believe it!"

"I can," said his mother.

The boy looked puzzled. "What do you mean?"

"Take out that penny I gave you and read what it says above Abraham Lincoln's head."

A radiant smile spread over her son's face as he read out loud, "In God We Trust!"

What are you putting your trust in? If it's material things, remember, they are only temporary. Instead, put your trust in God and His eternal life. He will never fail you.[1]

Fixer-Upper

But the people grew impatient on the way.
NUMBERS 21:4

R uth and Bob had purchased what is called in real estate terms a "fixer-upper." Though the roof leaked in a few places and the building had been neglected for years, the two-story house was structurally sound. They were unskilled in remodeling techniques, yet the real-estate agent assured them that with a little effort and some paint and wallpaper, they could make this dwelling a comfortable home. They bought the house.

The first room they tackled was the kitchen. They pulled off scarred countertops and unhinged cabinet doors. They scrubbed and scraped and peeled layers of dirt and accumulated paint and flooring. But two months later, with the kitchen stripped to the bare walls, Bob began a new job that required extensive travel time. The time he could spend restoring the kitchen was cut in half.

Ruth now washed dinner dishes in the bathtub and prepared meals on a two-burner hot plate while her country kitchen lay in pieces, scattered throughout the basement. Impatient to have her kitchen finished, she began to complain, at first just to Bob, but later to anyone who would listen.

The Israelites were a lot like that. When God set them on the road to the Promised Land, they weren't pleased with the route or the time it was taking to get to their destination. Rather than focusing their eyes on God and His plan, the Israelites looked at their circumstances and complained. A trip that should have taken a few days turned into a forty-year marathon.

As Ruth stood in the center of her gutted kitchen, God reminded her of the consequences of the Israelites' bitter attitude. With renewed determination, she quickly turned her impatience and discouragement into hope and thanksgiving by focusing on God instead of her kitchen. After apologizing to her husband, Ruth renewed her effort to help Bob pull the scattered pieces of their kitchen together until the job was finished.

In the same way, we can transform our "fixer-upper" lives with patience and a godly perspective. Do you have a room in your heart that needs a little "remodeling"?

Faith Moves Forward

"Men of Galilee," they said,
"Why do you stand here looking into the sky?"
A C T S   1 : 1 1

"**H**ey! Stop! The sink's going to overflow!" Ken's sharp cry alerted Ginny to the near disaster as he quickly came to her aid and turned off the water. "What were you looking at? Are the squirrels in the bird feeder again?"

Ginny had been staring out the kitchen window, gazing at nothing yet at everything all at the same time, oblivious to what was going on inside the house. "No squirrels. Just woolgathering, I guess," she replied absentmindedly.

She turned her attention to the dishes in the sink. For days she had been trying to make some sense out of the feelings that were swirling within her. Compared to someone else's problems, Ginny's concerns would seem to be only minor inconveniences, but for her, they were overwhelming. Finances. Relationships. Work. Health. Church. No matter where she turned, there were problems, and all of them seemed beyond her control. Tears mingled with the soapsuds as she finished the dishes. Drying her hands, Ginny sat heavily on a kitchen chair and whispered, "Lord, what am I supposed to do?"

And quietly, the answer came. When the disciples witnessed Christ's return to heaven, they stood gazing into the sky, not knowing what to do. They were paralyzed by the overwhelming responsibility that He had placed on their shoulders to share the gospel message with the world. It took a gentle shove from one of God's angels to get them moving down the path that had been placed before them, to turn them away from their fears and back to their faith as they followed God's plan for' their lives.

Sure enough, just like those disciples, Ginny had been paralyzed by her dread. She asked forgiveness for her fearful focus, and even before she reached the "Amen," she had a direction . . . a pathway. All she needed to do was faithfully follow God's plan. He'd take care of the rest.

What's holding you back from your God-given dreams? Are you afraid? Remember: Fear stands still, but faith moves forward!

Sacrifice at Sea

*I am the living bread that came down from
heaven. If anyone eats of this bread, he will
forever. This bread is my flesh, which I will give
for the life of the world.*
JOHN 6:51

Captain Eddie Rickenbacker, a famous World War I pilot, was forced down into the Pacific Ocean while on an inspection trip in 1942. The plane, a B-17, stayed afloat just long enough for all aboard to get out. Amazingly, Rickenbacker and his crew survived on rubber rafts for almost a month.

The men braved high seas, unpredictable weather, and the broiling sun. Night after night, they fought sleep as giant sharks rammed the rafts. But of all their enemies at sea, one was by far the worst—starvation.

After eight days at sea, all of their rations were gone or ruined by the salt water. They knew that in order to survive, they needed a miracle. According to

Captain Eddie, his B-17 pilot conducted a worship service, and the crew ended it with a prayer for deliverance and a hymn of praise. Afterwards, in the oppressive heat, Rickenbacker pulled down his hat and went to sleep.

"Something landed on my head," said Rickenbacker. "I knew that it was a seagull. I don't know how I knew, I just knew." He caught the gull, which was uncharacteristically hundreds of miles from land. The gull, which seemed to offer itself as a sacrifice for the starving men, was something Captain Eddie never forgot.

In the winter of his years, every Friday evening at about sunset, Captain Eddie would fill a bucket with shrimp and feed the seagulls along the eastern Florida coast. The slightly bowed old man with the gnarled hands would feed the gulls, who seemed to come from nowhere. He would linger awhile on the broken pier, remembering a time when a seagull saved his life.

Jesus offered Himself as a sacrifice, too. He is the Living Bread that came from Heaven. And just as Captain Eddie never forgot what one seagull meant to him, let's never forget what Christ did for us. Share the Bread of Life with those who are hungry.[2]

The Lost Ring

But godliness with contentment is great gain.
For we brought nothing into the world, and we
can take nothing out of it.
1 TIMOTHY 6:6-7

When Ginger lost the deep-blue sapphire ring that belonged to her mother, she was devastated. The sapphire, surrounded by twenty-three tiny diamonds, had been passed on to her after her mother died that November.

Ginger planned on having the ring sized to fit her smaller hand. For safekeeping, she placed the ring along with other pieces of jewelry into a plastic bag. Following the Christmas holidays, Ginger couldn't find the ring anywhere and soon forgot about it altogether.

As winter turned into spring, a friend planned a garage sale. Ginger decided to donate an old chest of drawers that she no longer needed. Afterwards, she realized that her mother's jewelry had been inside the chest of drawers, and it had been sold.

Fortunately, Ginger's friend had the phone number of the woman who had bought some of the jewelry. Relieved, Ginger called but was shocked when the woman denied having any of the valuable pieces.

Ginger was furious, and resentment began to build. Finally, her husband said, "Try to remember it was only a worldly possession. I know it's hard, honey but let it go."

With an aching heart, Ginger eventually turned the situation over to God and prayed for deliverance from her anger.

Two years passed. One day, the woman who bought the jewelry called and said her own mother had died. Suffering with back pain, the woman had been unable to attend her own mothers funeral. She returned the cherished ring to Ginger, as well as some of the other pieces of her mother's jewelry. Within a short time, the woman's back pain began to disappear.

How often we cling to material things! In Philippians 4:12, Paul says, "I have learned the secret of being content in any and every situation." We need to pray for contentment with what we have. It's a sure thing that we'll take nothing with us when we leave![3]

A Package or a Gift?

The gift of God is eternal life in Christ Jesus our Lord.

ROMANS 6:23

A festively-wrapped package rested on the kitchen counter. Having spent several days looking for just the right birthday present, Leslie knew her daughter would be pleased with the contents of the box. As she and her friends streamed through the back door after school, Leslie heard their exclamations—"Open it, Steph! It must be for you!"

Leslie joined the excited girls and smiled at the surprised look on her daughter's face. "It's so pretty, I almost hate to open it," her daughter said. "Maybe I should wait until later."

"No!" her friends cried, urging her to open the package immediately to see what was inside.

Armed with their encouragement, Stephanie grinned and tore off the wrappings. Prying open the small box, she gasped and quickly gave her mother a kiss. "It's just what I wanted!" she cried as she pulled the stuffed animal out of the tissue paper and showed the cuddly canine to her friends.

Stephanie's reaction reminded Leslie of the way she had been approaching God lately — hesitant to open the packages God wanted to give her every day. God offers us so many gifts — the gift of grace, the gift of peace, the gift of talents and abilities, the gift of love, the gift of eternal life. But all too often we stand and stare at God's packages and comment on how nice they are. We never accept the gifts as our own. We never open them to see what's inside.

Unopened, Stephanie's birthday present was just a pretty package. But when she accepted the present as her own and opened it, the package became a true gift from her mother's heart. With giggles and excited chatter, the girls disappeared to find the perfect spot in Stephanie's room for her newest stuffed toy. And Leslie opened her heart to receive the present God had for her — a gaily-wrapped package that became a gift of joy from God's heart to hers. Does God have a package waiting for you to open?

———————————

Survival Skills

For God did not give us a spirit of timidity, but a spirit of power, of love, and of self-discipline.
2 TIMOTHY 1:7

J ocelyn kept the food stamps hidden until all of her groceries had been rung up.

"That'll be $38.71," said the cashier.

Jocelyn's face turned red. She didn't look like the average person who used food stamps. She was dressed for an office job in a nice dress and heels. She felt people stare at her as though she'd done something wrong.

Embarrassed, Jocelyn pulled out the food stamps and paid for her order, then hurried through the door. At least if she'd had her children with her, maybe people would have understood. Even though she had a job, she still didn't have enough money to feed her family, and she felt ashamed.

That same year, she had needed emergency surgery for an ovarian cyst that kept doubling in size every two weeks. The doctors were afraid it was cancerous, while she was more afraid of the hospital bill. Explaining her dilemma to the doctor, she learned that the welfare system would cover her unexpected expenses.

The same week that Jocelyn needed surgery, one of her sons was hospitalized with what appeared to be spinal meningitis. The doctors refused to put off her surgery, and she ended up in a ward without even a telephone. With her eleven-year-old son in another hospital some fifteen miles away, she had never felt so alone. And because they were new to the area, there . was no one to talk to, or visit, her young son—not even her.

"Lord, I'm all alone," Jocelyn prayed. "Please help me to talk to my son."

When she told her doctor about her situation, he had her moved to a semi-private room where a phone waited beside her bed—all at the doctor's expense.

Are you in desperate need? Put your trust in our loving Father and boldly ask Him for help. He will take care of you.

———————————————

Kitchen-Sink Legacy

Do to others as you would have them do to you.
LUKE 6:31

Corinna's grandmother never went to seminary, but she sure could preach. From her kitchen-sink pulpit, Grandma would sermonize while she scrubbed the supper dishes. Her congregation of assembled relatives labored alongside her, clearing the table, drying the dishes, and putting away the pots and pans. Even the children were assigned after-dinner chores.

Corinna wanted to be like the neighbor children who gulped down their meals and left their dishes on the table as they flew out the back door to play. But Grandma would have none of that. If Corinna even hinted at wanting to be excused from her chores, Grandma would answer her with, "If you don't work, you don't eat." And then she would tell a story about how work wouldn't hurt her. By the time Grandma finished her sermonizing, it would be dark outside, and Corinna would have to wait until the next day to play with her friends. She quickly learned to do her chores without excuse or complaint; otherwise Grandma would remind her to "do everything without grumbling or complaining."

It seemed Grandma had a saying for every situation. If someone was upset about the treatment they had received from a friend, a clerk, or a neighbor, Grandma answered with, "Do to others as you would have them do to you." Or if she overheard one of the kids hinting that they were considering something naughty, Grandma quickly countered with, "Be sure your sin will find you out."

Only much later did Corinna discover that Grandma's gems of wisdom came from Gods Word. Jesus' words to His disciples were Grandma's answer to bad manners. Paul's words to the Thessalonians and the Philippians were Grandma's encouragement for her to do her chores without complaint. And Moses' words to the wandering Israelites were Grandma's disapproval of wrongdoing.

Grandma's example demonstrates that everyday chores can be used as an opportunity to share Gods love. Why not start a kitchen-sink legacy of your own and let your words — God's words — light the pathway for others?

The Quiet Touch of Stillness

In repentance and rest is your salvation, in
quietness and trust is your strength.
ISAIAH 30:15

A late-night snowfall blanketed the city one Saturday. When everyone awoke on Sunday morning, evergreens were layered with sparkling white icing. The roofs of houses looked as if someone had draped each one with a fluffy quilt. Lawns, sidewalks, and streets all blended into an unbroken sea of whiteness.

But more striking than the beautiful whitewash was the pervasive stillness. The city noises were gone. No horns honking or dogs barking. No traffic noise or boom boxes blaring. No doors slamming or machines running. Just stillness—quietness. It almost took your breath away.

The quiet didn't last long, however. Soon city snowplows were out, clearing and salting the streets. The sounds of shovels and snowblowers mixed with window scrapers and revving car engines as neighbors began to dig out from the storm. It was not the first snowstorm of the season, nor would it be the last.

But amazingly, that touch of stillness in the morning put everyone in a better mood. Even the coffee tasted better . . . richer . . . warmer. Despite the hard work of clearing the heavy snowfall, neighbors called out greetings to each other across the yards, accompanied by groans and laughter and squeals of delight. Adults and children made angels in the snow or engaged in mock battle in snowball fights. An entire family of snow people soon populated one lawn.

The quiet start to the morning left its imprint on the entire day The pace slowed for a moment, granting people an opportunity for reflection, allowing neighbors time to connect with others. And when normal activities resumed, some people were even able to hold on to the stillness for a while.

When Monday came, it brought with it all the noise of a busy week. But it also brought the remembrance of Gods words to His people—that in quietness and trust they would find strength. Let Gods quietness fill a corner of your heart today and find the joy that can be found in stillness. It's a blessing far better than a snowball fight!

Tending His Flock

He tends his flock like a shepherd: He gathers the lambs in his arms and carries them close to his heart; he gently leads those that have young.
ISAIAH 40:11

Eight-year-old Jonathan was always tempting fate. His mother often held her breath watching him climb to the highest branches of a tall pine tree. Swaying in the breeze, he'd call down to her, "Hey Mom, watch me!"

One day, Jonathan was riding his bike at breakneck speed downhill beside the house. At the bottom of the hill was his swing set, minus the swings. His mother watched in disbelief as her son raced down the hill, stood on the bicycle seat, then grabbed the top bar of the swing set.

She stifled a scream as he quickly flipped over the top of the bar and landed flat on his back on the cold, hard ground. It seemed to take forever for her to reach her son, who was uncharacteristically quiet. Gently, she lifted him in her arms, carried him back to the house, and placed him on the sofa.

Jonathan's chest ached, and he was breathing hard after having the breath knocked out of him. His mother wasted no time in dialing the doctor's office. While the pediatrician's phone rang and rang, Jonathan said, "Mom, I'm not hurt. I'm all right."

She began checking him for any sign of injury. Looking over his arms and legs, she was surprised to see where Jonathan had circled, with a ballpoint pen, every hurt, scar, scrape, or bruise.

"What is all this?" she asked.

Jonathan sat up on the sofa, beaming. "That's all my hurts. I put a circle around all of them," he said. Within minutes, he'd forgotten all about his pain, and after a bowl of mint chocolate-chip ice cream, he ran outside again.

Like a loving mother, God gathers His children up in His arms time and again, carrying us close to His heart. We may never know how many times God's providential hand has prevented an injury, either physical or emotional, in our lives. What a blessing to know He is ever tending His flock and protecting His lambs!

The Egg Test

As the heavens are higher than the earth, so are
my ways higher than your ways and my
thoughts higher than your thoughts.
ISAIAH 55:9

H ave you ever tried to read a recipe while you're cracking an egg into a mixing bowl? If you have—and you're not very adept at it—you know it's not a pretty picture. If you don't keep your eyes on the egg, you'll end up with more egg on the counter than in the mixing bowl. Sometimes you may miss the bowl entirely and the gooey egg makes a mess, running down the front of your kitchen cabinets, spilling onto the floor. Yuck! Any experienced cook will tell you that you'll have better success if you read the recipe first and then keep your eyes on the eggs.

The Bible agrees. Well, maybe it doesn't talk about eggs and mixing bowls, but it does talk about our choices in life. When the Israelites first camped on the edge of the Promised Land, God instructed them to do some reconnaissance. Twelve men were sent to look the land over and report back to Moses with their findings. All twelve had seen God miraculously deliver them from slavery. All twelve had heard God's promise of protection. All twelve had experienced Gods provision for their journey. But only two men remembered God and His faithfulness. Only two kept their focus on God; ten men were distracted by the sights and smells of Canaan. Ten men turned their eyes away from God and made a mess for the Israelites that took forty years to clean up. A glance away from God caused Israel's slippery slide to disobedience.

Whenever we focus on our problems instead of on God's promises and possibilities, we're in for a slippery slide, too. The Bible says that God doesn't view things from our limited perspective. If we want the recipe of our lives to turn out for the best, we need to stay focused on Him. Let the egg test be your reminder: Whenever you crack an egg for a recipe, keep your eye on the egg and remember to ask yourself if your heart is focused on God.

Send in the Clowns

Whatever you do, work at it with all your heart,
as working for the Lord, not for men.
COLOSSIANS 3:23

When the circus came to town, posters went up on the grocery store bulletin boards; billboards announced the performance dates, and television commercials urged listeners to "Come one; come all!" Lion tamers, wire walkers, and trapeze artists were part of the three- ring extravaganza. But the most anticipated performers were the clowns. With their crazy antics and outlandish costumes, they livened up each performance.

Clowns work hard at their profession. In fact, in order to travel with the Ringling Brothers Circus, clowns must successfully complete clown college—an intense course of study that covers everything from makeup to pratfalls, costuming to making balloon animals, juggling to sleight of hand. Only after clowns have mastered all of these skills can they take their place in the circus ring.

As Sheila stood at the stove sautéing vegetables for supper, she sensed a connection to this group of performers in the circus. Though she didn't wear a clown costume or clown makeup, she worked hard at juggling—balancing her time among home, family, work, friends, and church. She wasn't skilled at card tricks or sleight of hand, but she could work "magic," transforming everyday grocery items into flavorful meals seven days a week. And while she might not know the ins and outs of balloon-animal art, Sheila made lots of other things, from costumes for school plays to crafty Christmas gifts and decorated birthday cakes. And she had taken many a fall—not pratfalls, but real falls—when she'd gone inline skating with the children or walked the dog on icy sidewalks.

God's Word says that we are to work at whatever we do with all our hearts, remembering that whatever we do is for the Lord. Whether we're clowns or cooks, minstrels or mothers, we need to work hard at our profession. And when we do, we might just provide our friends and families with some laughter along the way!

Beauty for Ashes

[He has sent me] to bestow on them a crown of
beauty instead of ashes, the oil of gladness
instead of mourning, and a garment of praise
instead of a spirit of despair.
ISAIAH 61:3

S itting at her round oak kitchen table, Sharon smiled as she sprayed the glass in the frame with glass cleaner. The words of the inspirational poem she had written for a friend, who was facing cancer surgery, came into sharp focus. Later, Sharon would take her "food for the soul" to her friend.

Looking outside, the gray December day reminded her of a similar day when she was in seventh grade. That day, the sky was laden with gray snow clouds ready to give the world a new birth. She could still see her teacher standing at the chalkboard, asking the class to write a poem.

Aware that Christmas was at the doorstep, she began writing. Her poem, so different from those of her classmates, was about the birth of the Christ Child. She took it home and rewrote it until the poem shone as though it were the star of Bethlehem itself.

"This is wonderful," the teacher said the next day. "Did you do this all by yourself?"

Beaming, Sharon said, "Yes, ma'am." Then the teacher read the poem to the entire class. She was beside herself with joy that day.

A couple of days later, however, the teacher asked to speak to her in the hall. There, after talking to another teacher, she accused the child of stealing the poem from a book. Brokenhearted, Sharon refused to write another poem — until twenty-five years later.

By then, Sharon was a woman who had returned to writing as a form of therapy during some difficult trials. One day, with Christmas again approaching, she wrote several Christmas poems. She sent them off to a publisher, expecting a rejection. Later, she received a letter indicating that two of her poems had been accepted.

Are you neglecting your talents because someone criticized you in the past? Don't let your gifts become ashes; turn them into a crown of beauty for God. Bless others with your talent! Whether it's cooking, serving, speaking, writing, or making something beautiful with your hands, do it for His glory.

Perfect Landing

*She is clothed with strength and dignity; she can
laugh at the days to come.*
PROVERBS 31:25

B etty was normally a pretty good cook. She could prepare some delicious meals for her family, as long as they didn't want anything too difficult. One day however, her husband asked her to make biscuits for dinner. She had never attempted such a feat before, but with determination as her guide, she went to the grocery store to buy the ingredients. Luckily there was a recipe on the flour bag. As she gathered all the ingredients, she dreamed of the lightest, fluffiest biscuits ever.

When she arrived home, she preheated the oven, placed the ingredients before her and began the process of biscuit preparation. Everything seemed to be going fine, and soon she placed the baking dish in the oven. The biscuits even smelled great as they cooked. She was so excited that she called her starving family to dinner before she removed the biscuits from the oven. All the chattering kids sat down and placed their napkins in their laps. While she stirred the stew, she asked her husband to take the pan out of the oven and place it on the table.

Then everything got quiet. The kids looked at one another in disbelief, as their father shushed them with a glance. He followed his wile's instructions and placed the pan of biscuits on the hot pad. With an expectant smile on her face, Betty turned around to look. No one else was smiling. The biscuits were as flat as pancakes. Her family's eyes focused on her, waiting for an explosion of tears. Instead, Betty reached down and picked up a biscuit to examine it.

"What is that, Mom?" her youngest daughter asked.

"A Frisbee," she shouted, and sailed the biscuit across the room. Laughter broke the tense silence. The biscuits may have not been perfect, but the atmosphere was a joyful one as Betty's family enjoyed their mother's spontaneity.

The ability to turn a disaster into a comical situation is one we could all learn. There's enough in life to be serious about, so learn to laugh as often as you can!

Kitchen Sabotage!

God is not a God of disorder, but of peace.
1 CORINTHIANS 14:33

Kathleen's kitchen cupboards and drawers were a mess. Cupboards overflowed with mismatched dishes, receipts, expired prescriptions, and nearly empty bottles of cough medicine. Plastic storage dishes and lids seemed to be multiplying in the bottom drawer. Trying to find a wooden spoon in the drawer next to the stove was like going on a treasure-hunt. And odds and ends of twist ties, clothespins, and rubber bands cluttered the silverware drawer. There was no doubt about it. Her kitchen had been sabotaged by the excesses of daily life!

When her husband announced an upcoming camping trip, Kathleen sensed an opportunity to undo some of the damage to the kitchen. She helped pack food and swimming supplies, sleeping bags and flashlights, toys, and the clothes needed for a weekend in the woods. But when the time came for the car and camper to pull out of the driveway, she was not aboard. Her husband and daughter headed off for a weekend of fun and frolic while she turned back to the house to face the kitchen clutter monster!

Armed with cleaning supplies, trash bags, and new shelf paper, Kathleen surveyed the kitchen and mapped out her strategy. Soon she had unloaded the contents of the cupboards onto the kitchen table, the hallway floor, and the living room furniture. Time flew by, and she barely stopped to eat. But the interiors of those cupboards smelled fresh and clean, and the only items allowed back were things that were supposed to be there. Then she tackled the drawers.

When Kathleen tumbled into bed well past midnight, the cupboards were done. The drawers were organized. The counters were clear. Her body ached, but it felt good. She had taken a disorganized mess and made it into a useful kitchen once again. Now maybe she could find some time to spend with God.

Is there an area of your home or life that has been sabotaged by the excesses of life? Look for ways to set those things in order. The sense of accomplishment that accompanies your labor may even invigorate you for greater tasks!

Penny Bear

They will lay up treasure for themselves as a
firm foundation for the coming age.
1 TIMOTHY 6:19

I n the 1950s, a honey distributor packaged its honey in a glass bottle shaped like a baby bear. Grandma used this brand of honey in her cooking, and she quickly used up the contents of the uniquely shaped bottle. The bottle was too pretty to throw away, so Grandma put the bottle to use as a penny jar. Whenever Grandma found a penny on the sidewalk or received a penny in change, she would place those small copper coins in the bear-shaped bottle on her kitchen counter.

Her grandchildren loved to count the pennies in what they called Grandma's "penny bear." They'd pour the penny bear's contents onto the kitchen table and make neat stacks of pennies. Then they'd write the date and the total amount of pennies on a small slip of paper and tuck it into the penny bear's lid. Whenever the penny bear was full, Grandma took it to the bank and put the pennies in a savings account. The empty penny bear reappeared on the kitchen counter with a clean slip of paper in its lid. And so the process continued year after year.

When her oldest granddaughter began preparations for college, Grandma said she had something to give her. As she entered Grandma's kitchen, her granddaughter noticed a piece of paper sticking out of the top of the empty penny bear. She picked up the bottle and discovered that the paper was a check for the total cost of her books for her first semester at college.

Because of Grandma's penny-saving habits, there was enough money in the penny bear account to buy her college textbooks for that first semester and for several more years.

Now whenever her granddaughter finds a penny on the ground, she thanks God for Grandma's faithful stewardship. One penny is not worth much. But one penny multiplied can feed a hungry family, house a homeless person, or help a child through college. Little things do mean a lot.

Voice from the Past

*Faith by itself, if it is not accompanied by action,
is dead. But someone will say, "You have faith; I
have deeds." Show me your faith without deeds,
and I will show you my faith by what I do.*

JAMES 2:17-18

L aura was mixing cake batter when the phone rang. The voice on the other end said, "Hi. This is a voice from your past."

Since she didn't recognize the voice, Laura quipped, "Whose voice and from which past?"

Laughter broke out on the other end. "This is Carrie," she said. Of course, Laura thought. Carrie had been a member of her writer's group. In fact, Carrie had written beautiful and thought-provoking fiction. Her work was good, and she could have been published if she had pursued it. Instead, Carrie chose to end an unhappy marriage and get on with her life, leaving her writing far behind.

Carrie bubbled with excitement. "I'm sailing with friends on a forty-two-foot sailboat from Nova Scotia to Scotland."

Laura listened intently Was this the same Carrie who had needed lots of support from her friends? The same Carrie who had wrapped herself safely in a little shell?

To Laura's surprise, Carrie had changed. She was now taking control of her life and doing exciting things. She wasn't the least bit apprehensive about crossing choppy waters, battling seasickness, or running from sharks and killer whales.

As Carrie was closing the conversation, she said, "I wanted to make certain my good friends knew I was going on this trip."

Laura's breath caught in her throat. She had never thought of herself as Carrie's good friend. Sure, she'd taken Carrie to the doctor once, visited her apartment, and even lunched at a pizza place with her and her children, but she'd never thought.of herself as Carrie's good friend. She couldn't even recall Carrie's last name.

How often do we touch someone's life with a random act of kindness? God uses ordinary people to make an extraordinary difference in the world around them. Find a way to be kind to another person today.

Just Like Paul

Encourage one another and build each other up,
just as in fact you are doing.
1 THESSALONIANS 5:11

Prior to his conversion, the apostle Paul persecuted scores of Christians. But God met this ruthless Pharisee in a special vision on the road to Damascus and changed his heart.

Yet wherever Paul went after his conversion, he caused controversy. The book of Acts tells us that many Christians were unwilling to accept Paul's conversion as a real change of heart. They feared that his supposed love for Christ was mere playacting and would ultimately result in their imprisonment. Jews were angry at his new message, too. Death threats against him were commonplace, and the increasing threats of violence prompted the church leaders in Jerusalem to take Paul to the seacoast, place him aboard a ship, and send him back to his hometown of Tarsus.

For several chapters, the book of Acts is silent about the life of Paul. But when he reappears in the narrative in Acts 11, no one questions his change of heart. No one misunderstands his intentions. No one criticizes his involvement in missionary endeavors. Something is different about Paul.

While the Bible does not tell us what happened to Paul during that time, perhaps he went home to his family. Think of a time when you returned home after a long and maybe difficult absence. There's something reassuring about sitting at the same old kitchen table, cooking on the same old stove, listening to the same noises, and smelling the same aromas from your younger days—a simpler time. The four walls of the family home become a place to regenerate and renew. And when it comes time to move on again, you are refreshed and ready—just like Paul.

Whether you're sharing a favorite meal with a family member or a conversation with a friend until the wee hours of the morning, let your home be a haven . . . a place of refreshment. After all, you just might be strengthening another soul for ministry—someone like Paul.

Sunbeam Blessings

I am the light of the world. Whoever follows me
will never walk in darkness, but will have the
light of life.
JOHN 8:12

As Gloria sat alone at the dining table, a single sunbeam shone through the closed blinds. At the point where the light entered the window, it was just a tiny speck, but as it spread across the room, all the colors of the rainbow burst into an array of splendor. It highlighted the old shadowbox that hung on the wall and reflected on its glass front that protected her treasures from dust and grime.

The crystal ornament inside the box split the sunbeam into a million fragments of color and drew her attention to the other items. She spotted the golden tree figurine covered with her birthstones and thought of how her mother often spoke of what a glorious day it was when she was born. She saw the animal figurines that resembled her pets from long ago. The angel standing over the small boy and girl on the bridge reminded her of her childhood years, as she and her brother played by the creek's edge beside their home.

The baby figurine took her back to the days when her children were small. The fellow pointing to a carving in a tree that said, "I Love You," made her smile. It had been a gift from her husband on one of their anniversaries.

Many fond memories came alive as Gloria spied the tiny angel holding the Bible, and she thanked God for the many blessings in her life. Even in the midst of difficult circumstances, try to remember the good things God has done for you, no matter how small or insignificant. It will get your eyes off your problem and on the Solver of problems.

———————————————

Sweet Sleep

I will lie down and sleep in peace, for you alone.
O Lord, make me dwell in safety.
P S A L M   4 : 8

Are you a sound sleeper? Or do you sit up reading at your kitchen table late into the night? If you live near railroad tracks, you are probably used to the sound of trains and can sleep through the blaring of the whistle and the rumble of the engines. If you live near a fire station, you may be able to sleep through the sound of sirens. Some people become so used to the sound of their alarm clock that they have to find a new way to awaken themselves. Yet many people find it difficult to sleep soundly in stressful situations.

The apostle Peter probably was a sound sleeper. It seems that he could sleep soundly anytime and anywhere, day or night. The book of Acts tells us that Peter had been arrested for preaching the gospel. Though his friends had gathered together to pray earnestly for his release from prison, things looked bad for Peter. He was chained in a dark cell between two guards. But somehow Peter managed to fall asleep despite the uncomfortable surroundings. In the middle of the night, God sent His angel to rescue Peter. When the angel appeared in Peter's cell, the cell lit up with a supernatural glow. Yet Peter was such a sound sleeper that a light shining in his eyes didn't awaken him! The Bible says that the angel had to physically strike Peter on the side to wake him up. Once the angel had Peter's attention, Peter's chains fell off, and he escaped from prison.

We can be sound sleepers, too, despite hard times and stressful situations, if we learn what Peter knew well: God is in control. When we trust that God is in control of every aspect of our lives, we can "lie down and sleep in peace." Trusting in God's control is the best way to ensure sound sleep and sweet dreams!

Volcano Stew

Rejoice in the Lord always. I will say it *again:*
Rejoice!
PHILIPPIANS 4:4

C andy was running late again, and by the time she had climbed into her car in the parking lot, the streets were already clogged with rush-hour traffic. The leisurely, mid-morning, ten-minute drive home became a stoplight-ridden, horn-honking, thirty-minute commute. She finally stumbled into the house muttering apologies and grabbed the pot of leftover stew from the refrigerator. Slamming it on the stove, she flipped on the burner and rushed to change into some comfortable clothes while hollering, "Someone please set the table!"

A few minutes later when she rushed back into the kitchen, her nose sensed disaster. The stove! The pot of stew she had placed on the burner was a bubbling imitation of Mount Vesuvius. Tall columns of tomato-red sauce spurted into the air above the pot. Pieces of vegetables spewed over its sides. Apparently, in her haste to start supper, she had turned the burner to its highest setting, and now the stew was erupting all over the stove top.

Candy shrieked, and her family hurried into the kitchen. The pot was boiling so furiously that it was impossible to turn the burner off without being spattered by the tomato-sauce columns. The foaming vegetables were spilling over so quickly that no one could grab the pots handles without getting burned. But someone had to try. Amid exclamations of "Ouch!" "Hey, that's hot!" and "Yeow!" hands reached from all directions and eased the pot from its heat source.

Quickly Candy switched the burner off and surveyed the kitchen. Stew was splattered everywhere, and everyone's hands were covered with the sticky red goo. Her oldest child broke the silence. With a glint in her eye, she licked the stew from her hands and said, "Good dinner. Mom."

The laughter that accompanied the cleanup that night echoed with the Bible's admonition to always rejoice. If we have God's perspective on life, we can rejoice in everything — even volcano stew.

A Perfect Recipe

*An angel of the Lord said to Philip, "Go south to
the road – the desert road that goes down from
Jerusalem to Gaza." So he started out.*
A C T S   8 : 2 6 - 2 7

A story is told about a young bride who attempted to bake her first cake from scratch. The finished product was inedible, and the young woman sobbed her frustration to her mother. "I don't understand why it didn't look like the picture," she cried.

"Did you follow the recipe?" asked her sympathetic mother.

"Yes," replied the young woman. "I had to make a few substitutions though. The recipe said to use baking powder, but I only had baking soda, so I used that instead. And I didn't have baker's chocolate, so I used a candy bar. And I only had half the amount of flour, so I substituted extra sugar to make up the difference. And then Tom was due home early and I wanted the cake to be done, so I took it out of the oven when I heard his footsteps on the porch. Do you think it needed to bake for more than fifteen minutes?"

What the young woman failed to realize was the importance of following a recipe exactly as it is written. The proper oven temperature and time and the exact amount of specific ingredients, blended in the right way, will yield a picture-perfect result. Anything less than complete adherence to a recipe invites disaster.

God has a recipe for each of our lives, too. Our recipe will be a little bit different from another person's. One person may need more time in the oven of adversity than someone else. One may need more sweet experiences in life. Another may need the moisture of tears to soften a hardened heart. And still another may need more sunny yolks to brighten a dreary existence.

Only God knows the best recipe for our lives. Ask Him today to show you what He wants you to add to the recipe of your life, what He wants you to do, and where He wants you to go. If you follow His recipe exactly, the results of your life can be just like the one He pictured for you.

The God of Tomorrow

For I am the Lord - I do not change.
MALACHI 3:6 TLB

When the microwave buzzed, Rebecca slid her chair away from her laptop computer and retrieved the hot water for her tea. She had been writing an article about new technologies and how they would impact our lives in the next century. The whole topic was unsettling. The more research she did on the Internet, the more disturbed she became about cloning, supercomputers, and spy satellites. Where would it all end?

Suddenly, she had an urge to hear the comforting whistle of a teakettle, and the crackling of a real fire instead of the hiss of a gas log. The world was moving too fast, and at times like these, she wanted to crawl up in her grandpas lap and smell his sweet cherry pipe.

"Grandpa," she remembered asking one time, "did you have spaceships when you were little?"

He chuckled. "No, honey, when I was a little boy, we rode in a horse-drawn wagon to town. Airplanes had just really gotten off the ground."

"But you had trains."

"Yep, I guess I always liked trains the best."

The sound of a train whistle still reminded her of Grandpa and how he looked in his navy-blue conductor's uniform. Sometimes he would let her dress up in it and carry around his big silver watch. "All aboard!" she'd call, and Grandpa would pretend to be a passenger.

I wonder what Grandpa would think about life today? She knew. He'd tell her not to worry. "Honey," he'd say, "I've been in some pretty tight places in my day: train wrecks, labor strikes, and world wars. I reckon if God pulled us through all of that, He can see us the rest of the way home."

She "reckoned" He would. The God of her grandpa's era would be the same God in the twenty-first century. And that was a comforting thought.

Changing Seasons

*The grass withers and the flowers fall, but the
word of our God stands forever.*
ISAIAH 40:8

Marie had always enjoyed washing dishes by hand. It gave her an opportunity to slow down, think, and observe the changing of the seasons as she gazed out her kitchen window.

Over the course of a year, Marie watched a sparrow preparing her nest and then bringing food to her babies in the springtime. A hummingbird made regular stops after he discovered the window feeder during the summer. In autumn, squirrels scampered around in the crisp fallen leaves in search of an acorn. And that winter, Marie saw a deer standing majestically in her yard.

As the cycle of seasons began again, Marie watched flowers pop up through the soil when the weather got warmer. Their brilliantly colored blossoms always brought her happiness. In the summer, the green grass filled her heart with peace and tranquility. And as the green leaves gradually transformed to shades of gold, she sensed the autumn nip in the air, a sure sign that winter would follow.

Life is like the changing seasons. During the springtime of Marie's life, her days were filled with fun and joy as she played with frogs and tadpoles. Her teen and young adult years—the summer of her life— were marked by enthusiasm as she tried to find herself in the fast lane of life. Today, Marie is beginning to sense the contentment of autumn. She sees security in the eyes of her husband and joy in the lives of her grown children and realizes that winter soon will be upon her.

As a Christian, Marie knows that one day she will awaken to a world more wonderful than she can even imagine. Until then, she knows that whatever season she's in right now is the best season of her entire life.

There's nothing wrong with looking back at the previous seasons of our lives. But God has a purpose for allowing us to be in the season we're in right now. So enjoy where you're at on the way to where you're going!

Thank-You Notes

*Give thanks in all circumstances, for this is
God's will for you in Christ Jesus.*
1 THESSALONIANS 5:18

Most books on etiquette include several pages about the topic of thank-you letters. Many people feel that a phone call expressing gratitude for a favor, gift, or invitation is enough thanks. But most of us really appreciate receiving a short note in our mailbox that says thank you. It may contain only a few sentences. It may be typewritten or scrawled by hand. But just knowing that someone took the time to write a word of thanks for something that we said or did can leave a warm feeling in our hearts.

The person who receives the note is not the only one who is blessed. The one who sent the note benefits as well. When we take the time to sit down and collect our thoughts in order to put them on paper, we are actually taking time to dwell on the nature of the one who has done something for us. Quite often, because we have taken the time for that reflection, we find ourselves grateful for more than just one simple favor or gift.

The Bible says that we should be thankful to God "in all circumstances." We say thanks to God when we pray before meals. We often say thanks before we go to bed, too. But why not be different today and write a thank-you note to God? Do you have a roof over your head? Do you have food to eat? Do you have friends and family who love you? Thank God for those things. Is the sun shining today? Is it the beginning or the end of the week?

When you finish your note, date it, sign it, and put it away in the back of your Bible or in a favorite cookbook. You'll probably forget about it after a few days. But be assured that you'll find that note at an opportune moment, and you'll be reminded to say thank you again for the great things God has done for you.

Teenage Trauma

Charm can be deceptive and beauty doesn't last,
but a woman who fears and reverences God shall
be greatly praised.
PROVERBS 31:30 TLB

"But Mom, all the girls are wearing black lipstick," her teenage daughter cried.

"I don't care if they're wearing blue lipstick," Carol screamed. "You are not going out of this house dressed like a witch!"

Rachel stomped her foot and flounced out of the kitchen, and Carol winced as she heard her daughter slam the bedroom door. First it was miniskirts and a pierced nose, and now this. She fumed as she slapped mustard on a ham sandwich to take for lunch. What on earth was she going to do about that girl?

Remember when you wore miniskirts and white go-go boots? the still, small voice of God reminded her. Remember pale pink lipstick and bare midriffs?

Yes, Lord, she argued inside, *but You don't approve of her rebellion, do You?*

God seemed to answer, *I loved you even when you were yet in sin.*

Carol did love her daughter, despite Rachel's outrageous behavior . . . but she had to admit, she had done some pretty stupid things herself when she was her daughters age. Carol sighed. She didn't want to drive her daughter away like her own mother had done to her.

"Rachel," she said, tapping at the door. "Can we talk?"

"Go away!" her daughter sobbed.

"Please?" Gently, Carol opened the door and sat down on the bed beside her daughter. "I love you, you know. That's why I care so much."

Rachel rolled away from her mother. "All you care about is what your friends will say!"

"Right now, all I care about is what you have to say. Talk to me."

Every teenager is unique and special, yet every teenager needs the same things: love, discipline, and understanding. Start a dialogue with your teenager today.

Let's Try It Again!

A heart at peace gives life to the body.
PROVERBS 14:30

Misty held her big brother's hand in a vise-like grip. Her eyes widened as she took in the incredible scene playing out before her. There, atop the best sledding hill in all of Connecticut, her eighty-year-old grandmother was preparing for the ride of her life.

Poised on the toboggan, she sat as royalty, her long fur coat wrapped around her legs and her fur cap pinned perfectly into place. A small push on the snow with her elegant gloved hand . . . and she was off.

Halfway down the hill, the toboggan toppled to the side, and Misty watched in horror as her grandmother did an amazing acrobatic move through the snow, tumbling three times before sliding to a halt midway. Running full tilt to the rescue, Misty arrived breathless before a disheveled lump of fur.

Rosy cheeks appeared beneath a fur cap that was relocated to cover one ear. Snow was encrusted in the hair surrounding her face, and her bright, mischievous eyes met Misty's fearful gaze. With the confident laugh of one who loves God and knows of His care, Grandmother grabbed hold of Misty's hand. "Again! Let's try it again!"

That afternoon outing—followed by laughter and steaming mugs of hot chocolate around the kitchen table—made for one memorable winter day!

Whether it's an attempt at sledding for the first time in eighty years, or taking the hand of one you love and risking the exposure of your heart, God offers us the peace that brings comfort in the midst of life's chaos. In fact, it gives Him great pleasure. If we ask, God will give us the confidence to step into life's adventures, knowing that His hand will always be there to catch us.

———————————————

Realistic Expectations

The Lord has compassion on those who fear him;
for he knows how we are formed.
PSALM 103:13-14

"Watch out! Can't you be more careful?" It seemed like Jackie had been saying those words far too often to six-year-old Katie. This time her daughter's love of ketchup had resulted in a large tomato stain on a brand-new tablecloth. It had been a long day already, and Jackie's temper flared as the angry words escaped her lips. But as the words tumbled out, she saw Katie's quivering lip and a tear slip out of the corner of her eye.

Jackie felt terrible. Sure, the bottle had fallen over, but her daughter had not intentionally made a mountain of ketchup on the table. It was an accident.

Jackie had responded inappropriately and barked an angry response without thinking.

She stopped wiping the stain and reached across the table to give her child a hug. And then she looked her straight in the eye and said, "I'm sorry I yelled at you. Will you forgive Mommy?"

Her daughters tear-stained face nodded a reply, and they sat locked in a soggy embrace for several seconds.

Later, while finishing the dishes, Jackie thought again of the ketchup incident. And she thought about how much her daughter had changed since she was a baby. Katie could run and play and read and color and sing and laugh now, and Jackie expected so much from her at times. As Katie matured, her mother forgot too easily that she was only six years old. She often expected her to behave as if she were nine or ten.

Thankfully, God isn't like that. Yes, He has expectations for us. But God knows us and knows our needs. He readily forgives us when we get angry or do something wrong. He provides the things we need when we need them. He restores broken relationships and grants us wisdom and direction for living. But best of all, God remembers how He made us. And in His compassion, He never expects more from us than what He knows we can do or be.

Peace at Last

*Peace I leave with you; my peace I give you. I do
not give to you as the world gives. Do not let
your hearts be troubled and do not be afraid.*
JOHN 14:27

With a throbbing headache, Diane prepared breakfast for her children and made a mental note of all the people she needed to contact. Her aunt in the nursing home would love to have her stop by for a chat, as would her single neighbor down the street.

But she just didn't have the time! Diane pushed the boxed greeting cards out of the way to set down the cereal bowls and thought of a friend who had just lost her mother. A simple card could say so much.

Her thoughts were interrupted by the telephone. Her prayer partner told her that a man in their church had just suffered a heart attack. So many needs, and so little time!

"If only I had time to take care of all these things, Lord," she whispered, just as her kids ran into the kitchen arguing with one another.

"Please be quiet," Diane said. "My head is pounding."

In a few minutes, the kids were gone, and silence filled the house. Finally, she could rest. She turned on the television, then it dawned on her that this would be the perfect time to address a few cards and make some calls. She picked up the greeting cards and wrote down her thoughts. After addressing the envelopes, she picked up the phone and called the heart-attack victims wife. The report was good.

After a few minutes of prayer, Diane took a shower and realized that her headache had disappeared. She dropped her cards in the mailbox and briefly visited her aunt, who gave her a much- needed hug. Then she returned home and had the entire afternoon to clean house and prepare dinner, with enough left over to take a plateful of food to a lonely neighbor.

When she got home, Diane thought she had never felt better. God had given her the time she needed to take care of all the things that had weighed so heavily on her heart. And in giving, she had received far more than she ever expected.

At times, peace comes when we least expect it. But often, if we take notice, we'll realize that peace follows closely on the heels of reaching out to others.

At Your Age

Jesus Christ is the same yesterday and today and forever.
HEBREWS 13:8

One of the worst things about growing old is having your doctor preface all of his comments with, "When you get to be your age . . ." And when you get to be a certain age, you usually run headfirst into a brick wall called change. In fact, everywhere you turn you hear, "At your age, you're going to have to change . . . your eating habits . . . your diet . . . your financial goals . . . your sleeping habits." The list seems endless. But change is inevitable.

Many times the changes are for our own good. To lower our cholesterol count we need to switch to a low-fat diet. To ensure an adequate retirement fund we need to alter our spending and saving habits. To get a better night's rest we need to consider what we eat before we go to bed. To lose those extra pounds we need to change our exercise regimen.

While all of these changes may be necessary, they can be overwhelming. Scientists say that the process of change is one of the most stressful factors in human existence. So how can we incorporate these necessary changes into our lives without harming ourselves with increased stress levels?

Whenever possible, rather than throwing out everything familiar, we need to make changes to our lives in small increments. For example, if you have to move from a much larger house into a smaller one, make sure you take with you enough of those things that mean "home" to you, like your kitchen table or favorite wall hangings. Or if you have to make dietary changes for health reasons, see if you can still use your favorite tomato sauce to flavor that new tofu lasagna.

Also remember to think big. Think about God. Though things may be changing all around you, God never changes. He is still faithful, loving, forgiving, and caring. He is still strong, merciful, and trustworthy.

Face change by starting small, but thinking big. At your age, it's the only way to go!

A Balanced Life

I desire to do your will, O my God; your law is
within my heart.
PSALM 40:8

Henry tried with all his might to follow God. He attended church faithfully and served as a deacon. His mission, he felt, was ministering to the different families assigned to him, so several nights a week, he'd come home from work, take a shower, and leave to visit one of them.

On other nights, Henry attended meetings at church. He had a part in every program and every committee that the church sponsored. Being such a dedicated and well-informed man, the church looked to him for advice.

One night when Henry arrived home from work, his family was not there. He was appalled that his meal was not ready. How could he ever get to church on time if dinner was late? He went ahead and took his shower, hoping that his wife and children would be home soon. After another hour, they had not returned, so he finally left for his meeting.

When he arrived home later that evening, his family was already asleep. Upset, Henry awakened his wife and asked her where they had been and why dinner had not been prepared.

"We were at Keith's sports award banquet, honey. You were supposed to be there, too, remember?" she replied softly.

Henry hung his head. At that moment, he realized that he had neglected his own family while he was seeking to serve others for God. Yet his family had been patient and understanding with him.

The following Sunday, Henry resigned from most of his committees, discovering that he was more effective with only one church-related responsibility. He had learned to serve wisely without sacrificing the most important gift of all—the love and welfare of his family.

Unwanted Invaders

*See to it that no one misses the grace of God
and that no bitter root grows up to cause trouble.*
HEBREWS 12:15

Virginia's kitchen had been invaded. Not by ants or mice. Not by ravenous teenagers. But by moths. Just a few of them at first. But then, ten, fifteen, twenty a day. And not the big, fluttery kind of moths that hover around the porch light in summer. No, these were small, gray moths, barely a quarter of an inch long. Whenever Virginia opened a cupboard door, a moth inevitably flew out into her face. But where were they coming from? She had to find their hideout.

Systematically, Virginia's family began pulling open drawers and cupboards, finding small web-like nests that they washed away with disinfectant. After they had cleaned out all of the drawers and cupboards, the moth invasion slowed but never completely stopped. They could only assume that although they had wiped out some of the invaders' hideouts, there must be another stronghold somewhere.

With renewed determination, Virginia looked deeper for the source of the infestation, even checking behind the refrigerator and stove. But it wasn't until she saw a dead moth next to the dog's dish that she had her first real clue. They had recently purchased a new feeding system from a pet supply store, a container that held several pounds of dog food and distributed the food in measured servings into the dog's bowl. When she lifted the lid of the dog-food feeder and glanced inside, she knew she had finally found the source of the infestation and could once and for all get rid of the pests.

The Bible says that bad feelings can invade our lives like the moths invaded Virginia's kitchen. An unkind word or action can become the catalyst for long-term bitterness between two people. Unless the root problem for those bad feelings is removed, the relationship may suffer severe damage. But if we take the time to talk through the misunderstandings, we'll reap the benefit of a strengthened relationship. Open communication in a relationship will help close the cracks of bitterness and rid us of the infestation of hard feelings.

Monday Morning Mindset

Let us continually offer to God a sacrifice of praise.
H E B R E W S   1 3 : 1 5

On Monday, the television newscaster looked grim as he read the statistics of the latest crime spree. The weatherman predicted a heavy snowstorm with possible ice damage and power outages. The car mechanic indicated that the repairs to the brake system would cost more than expected. The doctors office called, requesting an immediate appointment to discuss the results of a biopsy.

But also on Monday, Grandma went to the oncologist and received a survivor pin commemorating five cancer-free years. Amy pulled through labor and delivery with no complications and gave birth to a healthy little girl. Sam's blood test revealed that he was merely overstressed and overtired, not diabetic. Frank passed a college exam with flying colors. Erin believed she had found someone to many.

All of these events are part of the routines of daily life and frame the conversations shared around the kitchen table. Sometimes those conversations are punctuated with sniffles and tears. But many times those talks ring loudly with laughter and song. The difference is usually found in our focus.

Concerns and problems are a part of life. Things go wrong. Plans fail. But we have a choice. We can either focus entirely on the problems or we can focus on God. A problem-filled focus yields a fearful heart, and fear is a thief that robs us of the joy of today. However, a focus that acknowledges God's control over everything fills our hearts with peace, comfort, and joy despite our problems. We can listen to the newscaster and the weatherman, the mechanic and the physician, but we need to make some time to focus on our daily blessings, too, thanking God for those little reminders of His care.

Rest assured, He is still in control of everything.
Tell Him about the heartache,
And tell Him the longings too,
Tell Him the baffled purpose
When we scarce know what to do.
Then, leaving all our weakness
With the One divinely strong,
Forget that we bore the burden
And carry away the song.

PHILLIPS BROOKS [4]

The Better Way

*Since, then, you have been raised with Christ, set
your hearts on things above where Christ is
seated at the right hand of God.*
COLOSSIANS 3:1

———————————————

Martha was a dedicated homemaker. She was an expert at entertaining her guests while preparing a scrumptious meal at the same time. One day when Jesus was passing through the village, Martha opened her home to Him. Her house was spotless, and the aroma coming from her kitchen was delightful. As a wonderful hostess, she made sure that Jesus felt welcome in her home.

Her sister, Mary, also was there. While Martha opened her home to Jesus, Mary opened her heart to Him and sat at His feet. She knew that true wisdom would be hers if she listened to His teachings and applied them to her everyday life.

Meanwhile, Martha began to grumble. She felt that Mary should be more involved in the work at hand.

She went to Jesus to ask Him to send her sister to help her in the kitchen.

Jesus' response probably surprised her. He taught Martha some things about priorities, while sharing with her a better way to serve Him. Mary, He said, had chosen the better way, and it would not be taken away from her.

What are the priorities in your life? Do you take time out of your busy schedule to read God's letter to the world? The Bible holds the key to successful living and abounding happiness. Is your prayer time an important part of your day? Jesus is always available to listen to you. God is never too busy to offer encouragement and love to His children.

While working and serving are vital parts of living, it cannot be the most important part. Seek God's guidance today through prayer and Bible study. The wisdom that you gain will benefit not only you but others as well, as your life serves as a shining example for Him.

A Creative Boost

Be glad and rejoice forever in what I will create.
ISAIAH 65:18

When Larry was a child, his mother followed a regimented schedule of housekeeping and menu plans. Monday was letter-writing day and meat loaf for supper. Tuesday was reserved for laundry and baked chicken. Wednesday was the day to help Grandma with her housework while a roast simmered in the oven. Every day had its own chore and its own menu. Though it was repetitive, the family always knew what to expect for dinner.

Lisa, however, had been raised in an unscheduled environment. Her mother's whim, coupled with the food in the cupboard, determined what a given night's supper would be. But when Larry and Lisa married, he wanted to know what she planned to serve for dinner every night. He was used to regularly scheduled menus and appreciated knowing what to expect. Lisa found such a schedule too confining; she wanted the freedom to be more creative.

They decided to compromise. Three days out of every week were set aside as pre-planned menu days. On those days, Larry knew what to expect for supper. The other four days were left to Lisa's discretion. Since she was a culinary novice when they married, that meant four days out of every seven Larry had to eat her experiments. Some were so bad they were inedible. But some were so good she still prepares them now, twenty-five years later.

Cooking and menu planning, along with many of the other responsibilities of homemaking, can become repetitive without the boost of a little creativity. Since God is our Master Creator, we can ask Him to show us how to be more creative in our cooking, in our housework, and in every repetitive area of our lives. It may be something as simple as eating our hot dogs and beans on the good china, but if we mix some of God's creativity into our everyday tasks, we'll find that a little "zippidee" in our "doo-dah" helps relieve the repetition every time!

_____

Soup Kitchen Compassion

*Putting the meat in a basket and its broth in a
pot, he brought them out and offered them to him
under the oak.*

JUDGES 6:19

Most American families eat a traditional meal at Thanksgiving: a turkey dinner with all the trimmings, followed by pumpkin and apple pies for dessert. Later that evening, everyone grazes on turkey leftovers, served as hot sandwiches with gravy or dipped as chunks into salad dressing or cranberry relish. Two days after Thanksgiving, the soup pot will find its way to the stovetop. Odds and ends of turkey, leftover scraps of vegetables, a handful or two of noodles, and a strange assortment of spices will blend with the dribs and drabs of leftover gravy to simmer on the stove, infusing the entire house with the aroma of turkey soup.

While the steam from the soup has been scientifically proven to benefit dry nasal passages, there's something more healing in that old pot of soup than mere steam. And while nutritionists tell us that a bowl of soup will help cut down our caloric intake of fatty foods, there's something more restorative in that boiling mixture than just a filling liquid. For many, that turkey soup is a symbol of caring and compassion.

For many years of our nation's history, the masses of unemployed workers far outnumbered those who were able to earn a living. During the Depression era, churches and civic organizations opened feeding centers, offering a bowl of warm soup to people who may not have eaten for days. Soup kitchens, as they came to be called, are still in existence, often ministering a message of God's love with a meal and warm shelter.

Our homes can serve as a place of warmth and shelter, too. All around us are people who are facing tough times, people who need to know that they are loved and appreciated. Probably within your own circle of friends, you can think of someone who needs an encouraging word or a shoulder to cry on. Why not let your kitchen become a soup kitchen of encouragement? Warm your friend with a cup of soup and a bowl of love today!

Someone Who Cares

*But when you give to the needy, do not let your
left hand know what your right hand is doing, so
that your giving may be in secret. Then your
Father, who sees what is done in secret, will
reward you.*
MATTHEW 6:3-4

Maureen wearily rinsed out her coffee cup and stacked it in the nearly full dishwasher. Her life had been difficult for months. As her husband's illness rapidly progressed, her sense of security waned and a fear of losing him filled her heart. After a few weeks in the hospital, her husband of forty-five years was forced to live in a nursing home. It seemed that Maureen couldn't stop crying. Her heart felt heavier after each visit.

At first, people asked if there was anything they could do to help. Others telephoned and visited her. But after a few weeks, the calls and visits dwindled as her friends got on with their lives. She was overcome with weariness, and joy seemed so remote.

One day before she left for her daily visit to the nursing home, she stopped by the mailbox. A small "thinking of you" card was tucked inside. It was signed, "Someone who cares." A ray of sunshine touched her heart as she read those simple words.

Someone really cares, she thought. She didn't know who it was, but she knew that someone was concerned about the situation that overshadowed her life. All day long she wondered who had been so kind. She looked at the card over and over, trying to see if she could recognize the signature. She knew that the person was praying for her, and she wanted to let her know how much she appreciated it.

As the weeks and months passed, Maureen continued to receive greeting cards from this anonymous person. The signature was always the same. But no one ever confessed to being the sender. Only God knew who uplifted her spirit. And for the sender, that was enough.

The Junk Drawer

The good man brings good things out of the good stored up in his heart, and the evil man brings evil things out of the evil stored up in his heart. For out of the overflow of his heart his mouth speaks.

LUKE 6:45

"Honey, where's that little hammer I use to hang pictures?" Carl yelled from the bedroom.

"Look in the junk drawer," Cathy replied automatically, as she stuffed laundry into the machine. She heard Carl muttering and shuffling through the bottom drawer in the kitchen.

"There it is. Hey, I forgot I had this!"

Soon she heard her husband whistling and tapping a nail into the wall. Sighing, she pushed the drawer shut with her foot. They had been married for twenty-three years, and everywhere they went, the junk drawer went with them. She couldn't even remember when they didn't have one.

Need some tape? Look in the junk drawer. How about some nails? Try the junk drawer. Old keys, hooks, two-sided tape, pushpins, ballpoint pens, short pencils, and other assorted gadgets or parts, whose origin had long faded from memory, followed them from house to house. While some of the disorganized stuff was useful, much of it could have been thrown away long ago, and a few of the items could be downright dangerous in a child's hands. For years, they had talked about cleaning out the drawer and throwing a lot of it away. But that chore was always last on the list of other priorities.

It made Cathy think about her relationship with God. It was so easy to postpone her devotions or let the day crowd them out altogether. Yet she had to admit that she always had time for her favorite television shows. What was she storing up in her heart? Good things? Useless things? Even dangerous thoughts? Was she carrying around habits that she would be better tossing out with the rest of the trash? It had been a long time since she had taken inventory of her life.

With a determined tug, Cathy pulled out the heavy junk drawer and set it on the counter, and by the time she finished going through it that Saturday afternoon, everything had been returned to its proper place or found a home in the trash. Tomorrow, she vowed, I'll start on myself.

___

A Lot of Fries

"Bring the whole tithe in to the storehouse, that
there may be food in my house. Test me in this,"
says the Lord Almighty, "And see if I will not
throw open the floodgates of heaven and pour out
so much blessing that you will not have room
enough for it."
MALACHI 3:10

Four-year-old Billy could hardly wait. In his small world, a burger and fries were pure Heaven. When his father arrived home with the precious bag in hand, Billy was thrilled. It had been two whole weeks since he had smelled that luscious fragrance. He quickly tore into the sack and popped a french fry into his mouth.

"Billy, may I have one of your fries, please?" his dad asked.

Billy looked up at his father, an expression of disbelief and then horror crossing his face.

"But Da-a-d," he whined with convincing pain. "They're mine!"

His father looked at him with open surprise. "Billy, who bought you those fries?"

With his head down, he answered, "You did."

Ever feel like Billy? Like young children reveling in the abundance of their parents' resources, we turn to God and say, "But it's mine!" when He asks us to give. Our time, our talents, our money, our heart, and our love all have been given freely to us. It should be a pleasure—a real joy—to return a small portion of something that never belonged to us in the first place.

Imagine walking into a church and having someone hand you a hundred dollars. In the middle of the service, the ushers take up a collection and ask you to contribute ten dollars. Wouldn't you joyfully give such a small portion of what you had received? When God blesses us, it is a pleasure to return the favor. Sing, play, dance, write, and give back to God part of what He has given you.

He promises that when we offer a portion of it back to Him, He will "throw open the floodgates of heaven and pour out so much blessing that you will not have room enough for it."

As Billy would say . . . that's a lot of fries!

———————————

Spiritual Physics

He who walks with the wise grows wise.
PROVERBS 13:20

"Mama!" Josh's voice carried through the quiet house.

"Yes, Josh?"

"Mama! Come bounce me!"

Mary looked out the kitchen window to the trampoline that seemed to take up half the yard. With a smile that dimpled her cheeks, she grasped her youngest sons hand and went out to bounce him. It was an odd sort of pride she took in being able to skyrocket her sons little body into the air. She outweighed him by a number of pounds, and her weight caused him to go higher than any of his friends could take him. It was just a simple matter of physics, really; the heavier your partner, the higher you go.

It's no different spiritually. The people you surround yourself with will either send you skyrocketing into spiritual understanding and maturity or leave you grounded and struggling.

When you look at those in your life today, who is it that stands out as wise? Who walks with that quiet charisma and peace that you find yourself craving? What would it take to call that person? Keep it simple and comfortable. Plan a casual lunch at home, invite her over for coffee, or simply spend an afternoon talking. Or perhaps you can find an activity you both enjoy. Surround yourself with people who will encourage your growth.

The Bible says in James 1:5, "If any of you lacks wisdom, he should ask God." Ask God to expand your wisdom and your world.

A Continual Feast

*All the days of the oppressed are wretched, but
the cheerful heart has a continual feast.*
PROVERBS 15:15

———————————————

J anice could barely look at Minnie. She saw in the aging, lined face before her the haunting call of her own weary bones. Working in a nursing home when she herself was growing older could sometimes bring a deep sadness to Janice's heart. And here she was, watching the end of a life struggle to move down the hallway.

Minnie, Janice's patient, was bent at the waist and shuffling slowly with the use of a walker. Her stiff and gnarled hands were white with the pressure. It took Minnie what seemed like hours to make her way across the small expanse of tile.

Finally, with much effort and painful exertion, Minnie turned and settled into the seat. Janice folded up the walker and leaned it against the wall, feeling her own aches and pains as she did so.

"Janice?" Minnie's voice was barely above a whisper as she beckoned Janice closer.

"Yes, Minnie?"

"Isn't it a beautiful day?"

Janice followed Minnie's line of vision, trying to see what beauty Minnie saw. There was little to notice: a plant, a painting, a few friends. Janice looked into her eyes. They were bright and capable, even though her body no longer followed suit. Minnie knew exactly what she was saying when she commented on the beauty of the day. Janice had to smile.

"Yes, Minnie, it's a beautiful day."

Is there an ache or pain you can set aside today to see the good? Is there something that's holding you back? Something that seems insurmountable? When you look beyond your circumstance, is there beauty there? Pain is real, and it's a struggle when life doesn't cooperate with our plans. But always, there is more. Always, there is something that God will place into our line of vision that is worth celebrating. It doesn't always take away the pain, but as He promises in Proverbs 15:15, "The cheerful heart has a continual feast." Once you start noticing the sublime, He makes it far too good to ever pass up again.

Hide and Seek

Then Barnabas went to Tarsus to look for Saul.
ACTS 11:25

W hen Lucille's children were young, they enjoyed playing hide and seek in the dark. The old country kitchen with its cavernous cupboards and deep recesses contained many good places to hide. On one such occasion, one of their cousins' — the smallest one, in fact — curled up into the back of the cupboard where Lucille kept her baking pans. When the pans were moved close to the cupboard door, the child was virtually invisible behind them. It was an ideal hiding place.

With a shout of "Ready or not, here I come!" the game started. One by one, the hiding places and hidden children were found. But the littlest cousin, curled up in the baking pan cupboard, evaded discovery. An older child would have been thrilled at not being found. But this child didn't see things that way. Sipping a cup of tea in the darkened kitchen, Lucille heard a tiny voice whimper, "Isn't anyone going to come looking for me?" That little voice was all it took for the rest of the children to locate their cousin. Though the others congratulated him on his hiding place, he was just glad someone had found him.

Though Paul wasn't playing hide and seek, the Bible tells us that he had been hidden in Tarsus for quite some time. He could have easily felt abandoned by the other believers. He could have wondered if anyone even cared to know where he was. But then God sent Barnabas to find Paul. And when Barnabas found him, the two of them began a missionary journey that would ultimately change their world for Christ.

Though we may not play hide and seek anymore as grown-ups, we can sometimes feel buried under responsibilities and schedules that close in on us and hide us from time with friends and family. That's when we need someone like Barnabas—someone to seek us out and show us that they care.

Do you know someone who needs a Barnabas? Reach out—with a note, a phone call, a prayer, or a visit—and do a little seeking, not hiding, today.

Cardinal Grace

Give me a sign of your goodness, that my
enemies may see it and be put to shame, for you,
O Lord, have helped me and comforted me.
PSALM 86:17

While Donnas six-year-old granddaughter fought the cancer that had invaded her brain, Donna often was amazed at Jennifer's child-like faith. Jenny had no doubt that God loved her and watched over her. Donna always accompanied her daughter and Jennifer to the hospital for the chemo treatments, and when they returned home, they would always stop in the city park for a few minutes. Even though the treatments made her nauseous, Jennifer wanted to drive the long way home to see the beautiful spring flowers, but she especially liked to watch the robins, bluejays, and cardinals. The cardinals were her favorite, she said, because red was her favorite color.

After Jenny's last chemo treatment, the doctor confirmed what they feared most of all. She only had a short time to live. When Jenny was not in a drug-induced sleep, she would tell her grandmother about the cardinal that frequently perched on her windowsill. No one but Jenny ever saw it.

Several months after Jenny passed away, Donna stood crying at her sink, feeling as cold and barren as the winter landscape. Her grief clung to her like a shroud. Why God? she cried as she had so many other times. Just then, a flash of red startled her. A cardinal! Fascinated, Donna watched as the most beautiful cardinal she had ever seen perched on the kitchen windowsill and cocked his head at her. Her tears stopped, replaced by the warmth and assurance of God's love. A moment later, the cardinal took flight and disappeared.

For days, the cardinal visited her every morning, and she found her heart growing lighter. Every day brought a cherished memory of Jenny's laughter, and Donna knew without a doubt that her granddaughter was happy and greatly loved by God. And she knew that one day, she would see her again.

Are you mourning the loss of a loved one? God wants you to know that He loves you and He sees your tears. Let Him comfort you today.

Do You Promise?

*The Lord is my light and my salvation - whom
shall I fear?*
PSALM 27:1

S amantha had to have the promise. Every night at bedtime, Sam always called out to her mother as she walked away from her closed bedroom door: "Mom? Do you promise?"

"Yes, honey, I promise."

Every night, she and her mother said the same words. Their ritual began with Samantha's fear of tornadoes, then dogs, then the green-eyed slime monster that she had glimpsed on a television show she wasn't supposed to be watching. Fear of snakes, the boogeyman, thunderstorms, fire ants (her mother is still not sure what brought that one on!), winged creatures of every sort, and fires followed one after another. Especially fires.

But later, the promise was no longer specific . . . just the general promise that Sam would wake up whole, unscathed by alien dream creatures, and free from wounds inflicted by nature.

Her mother took a risk every night, promising that no harm would come to her young daughter. The truth was, a thunderstorm could occur, a fire ant could crawl into her bed, and even a tornado was not beyond the realm of possibility.

But in another sense, there was no risk. The Bible says that there is no fear in Christ Jesus. He is the snake killer, the thunderstorm tamer, and the water that douses every fire. He annihilates the boogeyman, and there is no winged creature that could escape His wrath. With God on your side, there is absolutely nothing to fear! It's tough to fathom, but so important to grasp. When our heart rests with Him, there is no one who can break it. When our aching body cries for help, He is there to grant us peace. Even in the face of death, He brings life to the darkness. There is no caging His protective presence. Cast off your fear; He will take it and tame it. For His promises can never be broken!

Wrong Route

*Wait for the Lord; be strong and take heart and
wait for the Lord.*
PSALM 27:14

Downtown Seattle . . . sitting in the hotel lobby and waiting for a bus. Lizzy and Karen had broken free of a conference and were ready to explore the city that surrounded them. They'd been waiting for the bus for twenty minutes and found themselves impatient and eager. There was so much to do . . . so much to see!

Moments later, a bus pulled up. "It's not the one they said we should take," Lizzy said, smiling as she began walking toward the doors, "but it's headed in the same direction! Let's go!" They climbed on board— two Midwestern girls, heading for the sights. As the bus made its way through the dark and scary underbelly of the city, the girls huddled together in a small corner of the bus. The driver seemed amused by their predicament, and their fellow passengers seemed anything but willing to help them find their desired destination. They grasped each other's hands and tried to look less like tourists and more like residents. That only served to emphasize their discomfort.

Lizzy and Karen ended up staying on the bus for the whole route. Arriving back at the hotel, they were slightly shaken and had only lost a little time. They grinned at each other ruefully and waited . . . and waited . . . and waited for the right bus.

Is there a bus you're tempted to climb aboard because you're tired of waiting? Is there a relationship, a job, a direction you're thinking of taking that may not be God's best for you? There is much to be gained by waiting in the lobby for the right bus. God will not abandon you in your search. He is there, ready and waiting with His answer, reminding you of His sovereign will and His ability to take you where you need to go. It's okay to wait on Him. In fact, it's much safer and a whole lot wiser, especially when you consider the alternative.

The Gift of Words

There are different kinds of gifts, but the same Spirit. There are different kinds of service, but the same Lord.

1 CORINTHIANS 12:4-5

Melissa wanted more than anything to be able to sing and play the piano! Unfortunately, she simply had no musical talent, no matter how hard she tried or how much she practiced. She finally came to the conclusion that she had no sense of rhythm and no ability to carry a tune.

Marrying a preacher with a beautiful voice didn't help matters. Everyone knows that the pastor's wife is supposed to play the piano. She had never seen it written in any book, but she saw it written on ever)' church member's face. She hated pastoral interviews, because she knew the dreaded question would come eventually: "Do you play the piano?" She always felt like a failure as she answered that inevitable question with a solemn no.

For years she prayed, "God, give me the ability to sing," but during the congregational hymns, she realized that nothing had happened. Her voice was just as bad as it was before she prayed. She took piano lessons until a well-meaning teacher kindly told her that she was wasting her money. Many times she wondered why God didn't answer her prayer in the way she would have liked.

One day, Melissa started singing for the joy of it and gave up on the idea of being an accomplished pianist or soloist. She sang in the shower after everyone had left for the day and hummed as she cooked before anyone arrived back home in the evening.

She taught Sunday school and later started writing. She discovered the talents that God had given to her had nothing to do with music. He had given her the gift of words. Melissa worked hard at becoming a successful writer and reached many people with her words of encouragement.

God does not give everyone the same talents.

We're all unique and special in His eyes. Discovering her talent gave Melissa an entirely different outlook on life. Now when that difficult question arises, she smiles and answers, "No, I don't sing or play, at least not for anyone except the Lord! Instead, He gave me the gift of encouraging others."

Nowhere to Hide

*Where can I go from your Spirit? Where can I
flee from your presence?*
P S A L M   1 3 9 : 7

"How did you know I was here?"
Patty rested her head against the
steel post of the bridge and swung
her legs gently over the water below.

"Where else would you be?" her husband, David,
asked. He stood behind her, respecting her need for
space. "This is where you always come when your
heart hurts. After three years, you don't think I know
that?"

Patty beckoned him to sit beside her. "In a way, I'm
glad you know." He sat down. "I come out here to be
alone, but I don't really want to be alone. Part of me
needed you to know . . . to search and find me. I
wanted to know that someone cared enough to worry

about how I was doing." She paused. "I guess that's silly, huh?"

David took her hand in his. "No, it's not silly." He said nothing else. He just sat there, quietly supporting and loving her, knowing she needed to be alone but not alone, separate but still loved.

Our Heavenly Father knows us even more intimately than our own spouse. When we try to run and hide from God's presence, He is always there — not as an intruder or an accusing presence, but as a loving companion. He is a friend who holds us even when we're afraid to look Him in the eye. His love knows no hiding place. There is nothing to run from if we belong to Him. So often He won't speak a word when we try to escape Him. He just waits, acknowledging our choices and loving us just the same.

Have you run away from your Father? He is there if you want to talk to Him. He knows your heart, and He wants to be with you. Even in the moments of aloneness, God is your silent companion.

A Soothing Lotion

As a mother comforts her child, so will I comfort you.
ISAIAH 66:13

Anne felt bloated. The pain from her incision was excruciating, worsened by the hacking cough she could not seem to shake. Her husband was at work, and her new daughter was sleeping soundly in her crib. In the moment of silence, she tried to absorb the peace that seemed to surround her but remained far from her grasp.

Anne's mother sat beside her, her dark brown eyes comforting and understanding as she read the restlessness and frustration in her daughter's face. Anne had been home from the hospital for just forty-eight hours, yet her doctor had prescribed six weeks of recovery time after the emergency caesarean section. Anne struggled not to feel sorry for herself. It was difficult, though. Her distant husband seemed cold and uncaring, her home was in a shambles, and her pain unbearable.

Anne continued to wallow in her misery and barely noticed as her mother knelt before her and gently removed the socks from her swollen, hurting feet. Her mother took one foot in her hands and began to rub it in a smooth, rhythmic motion. The pain lessened. Anne started to notice.

As she watched her mother's aging hands soothing her swollen ankles, applying lotion to the dry areas, and massaging the calluses, Anne marveled. Her mother's hands were strong and tenacious, characteristic of a woman who had held her own in every aspect of life. Anne glanced down at her own tender hands. They were still plump with youth—full and unlined. They didn't have the marks of wisdom, the edges of strength, or the grasp of one who labors. The one she should serve was serving her.

Just like Jesus washed the feet of His disciples before the Last Supper, God serves us, comforts us, and holds us in His arms in the midst of confusion. He assures us through His Word that He will be there to comfort us in the midst of life's chaos, even more than a mother comforts her own child. Rest in that knowledge today. Let it be a soothing lotion to the dry and barren patches of your soul.

Better Things in Mind

Because the Lord disciplines those he loves, as a father the son he delights in.

P R O V E R B S   3 : 1 2

"**Y**ou just don't want me to have any fun!" Dell slammed out of the house and stomped through the backyard. He had no idea where he was going and no way to get rid of his anger, and he was a little nervous that he might be acting childish.

Dell hated the control his parents exercised over him. His friends got to do whatever they wanted, and no one cared. They could stay out late and watch whatever movies they wanted, and some of them were dating already. At fourteen, Dell felt he should have the same privileges. What made those other kids so special? Why didn't his parents trust him?

"Dell?" It was his dad. For a moment, Dell was tempted to ignore him, but he couldn't find the resolve. He turned around reluctantly.

"What?" he asked. He almost missed the football flying through the air and had to quickly throw up his hands to block it. "Geez, Dad!"

He held the pigskin in his hands, tempted to toss it aside. But there was his father, waiting patiently, a smile on his face. Dell swallowed his anger and tossed the ball back. He supposed there could be worse things than having a father who tossed a football around with him, a dad who wanted to keep him pure of heart so that he would do what was right.

How often do you find yourself storming away from God's presence, holding onto something that He has asked you to let go of? How often do you resist His authority because of what your friends are doing? We are not so different from that young teenager, straining for independence. We need to keep in mind that the Father who corrects us knows where we are headed. He wants to keep our vision unclouded so He can lead us to the life He has set aside for us. Allow God's correction to be the greatest affirmation of His love and hope for your life.

What's Wrong, Honey?

For everyone who asks receives; he who seeks finds; and to him who knocks, the door will be opened.
MATTHEW 7:8

Phyllis will never forget the day God answered one of her prayers in a miraculous way. Pregnant and at home with her two children, Phyllis had no means of transportation. Her husband, Carl, worked on the road and was driving their only car. She had no idea where he was, and as much as they wanted one, they could not afford a cellular phone.

The morning was going well for Phyllis. Her five-year-old twins played in their room while she cleaned house. Around lunchtime, she heard a loud thump. Just as she got to their bedroom door, she saw one twin sail off the top bunk. They had been warned not to play up there, but their desire to fly was just too great. The first twin had landed safely, but the second broke his arm, learning the hard way that little boys

Carl wouldn't be home for several hours, and since she couldn't reach him, she immediately called her father, to take her and the children to the hospital. She cradled her screaming son while waiting for her dad. It then dawned on her that if she didn't write a note, her husband would come home to an empty house. But if he found a note, saying they were at the hospital, he would think something had gone wrong with the pregnancy. Crying out to God, she asked Him to have Carl call home. Just as she said, "Amen," the phone rang.

"What's wrong, honey?" Carl asked. For several seconds, she was speechless.

"How did you know something was wrong?" she asked.

"I just had a feeling," he said. After she told him the news, her father arrived. Carl met them at the hospital.

Phyllis was thankful that her line of communication to God was open and that He immediately relayed the message to Carl, saving them both a lot of fear and worry. That line is always open. But you have to call first! Today, sharpen your communication skills by spending some time in prayer.

_____

Guilty Snacking

Watch and pray so that you will not fall into temptation. The spirit is willing, but the body is weak.

MARK 14:38

Stacie was sitting in her office when she first heard the commotion.

"No way!"

"Check it out!"

"Who's got some quarters?"

Stacie got up from her desk and walked cautiously toward the sound of money and elation. She rounded the corner to discover three of her co-workers gathered around the vending machine. They were inserting change, picking out items, and receiving both the snack and their money back. The machine had a loose wire and was giving out free food.

Stacie grinned. No breakfast that morning and quarters in her pocket made for a happy young woman. She pushed her way through the crowd and gave it a try. Three quarters . . . some powdered donuts. Three quarters back . . . a big cinnamon roll. Three quarters back . . . a bag of chips. Carrying her quarters and her unexpected breakfast, she headed back to her desk with a smile on her face.

It wasn't until she sat down that the guilt (and the calories) settled heavily on her conscience. It wasn't right! No matter that everyone else seemed to be okay with it. No matter that the vending machine guy was always grumpy and never stocked the items she liked . . . no matter about any of that! This was wrong. It was stealing, and she couldn't do it.

Oh, but how her stomach growled! Surely it would be okay if she had one bite . . . just one.

Stacie ate it all. But when the vendor came later, she dug into her pocket and paid for all three items. Her coworkers looked at her oddly, but she felt much better.

Sometimes it's easier to ignore the little things that no one else cares about—to join others who believe that if no one knows, it can't possible hurt. Today, take a stand for the little acts of truth . . . the small steps of honesty and courage. Though some may mock you, you just may earn the respect of others, and God will use that to draw them to His heart.

———————————————

Playful Joy

[There is] a time to weep and a time to laugh.
E C C L E S I A S T E S   3 : 4

Grandma Lu watched her grandson, a bit perplexed by his actions. Benjamin, in all his six-year-old glory, was spinning. Not for any apparent reason, he was simply spinning, around and around and around. His little arms were stretched out on either side of his body, and his head was thrown back as a deep belly laugh escaped from his rosy lips. It didn't seem that he was doing much . . . hardly anything amusing or interesting.

Grandma Lu paused.

Was there something fun about spinning? She glanced around the lobby of the hotel where she sat. There were only a few people nearby and they were buried deep in magazines and newspapers. She stood up and set her purse on the seat, blushing even as she walked toward her spinning grandson. She wasn't sure if there was any special technique, so she watched him for a moment before spreading out her own arms. She began slowly at first, careful not to bump into anything, worried she might slip and fall. Then she threw caution to the wind and began to speed up. She threw her head back and laughed, and felt the momentum of her own body carry her in circles. What fun!

A few minutes later, she slowed to a stop. Benjamin stood before her, his mouth open, his eyes wide. He began to laugh, and she laughed with him. They made quite a pair in that hotel lobby — disheveled, flushed, spinning grandmother and grandson. But people smiled, because their joy was real.

Laughter is Gods gift of healing for a saddened heart. It gives lightness to the spirit and gets the blood flowing. Find a way to laugh today; rent a funny movie, read the comics, or play with a child and forget you're an adult. Do things you wouldn't normally think of doing and allow yourself to enjoy it. There is a time to laugh. Take that time today and revel in the abandonment of playful joy.

Monster Hugs

Be glad and rejoice forever in what I will create.
ISAIAH 65:18

"That's thirty-four monster hugs, Mommy!"

Sandy tugged on her mother's shirt and pointed to the chart on the refrigerator. "Yup! Since I did my room, that's three, and then I was nice to our guests, that's five . . . and then I get an extra five for being your favorite daughter!"

"You're my only daughter, Sandy!" her mom laughed.

"Yes, but that should be worth at least five!"

Sandy smiled at her mother in that mischievous way and wrote "34" at the far end of the chart. Her mother didn't stop her. Why begrudge her five monster hugs? They were a pleasure to give. She picked up her daughter, who at age seven was getting harder to lift, dropped her on the couch, and kissed, giggled, and cuddled—each monster hug lasting about thirty seconds. Every time her daughter did something well, she earned monster hugs. Not only were they a pleasure for Sandy, but they were a joy for her mother, an incentive that tied their love together.

How much more does our Father in Heaven wish to reward us for steps in the right direction! It is as much a pleasure for Him to give as it is for us to receive. He enjoys blessing us. He knows our greatest pleasures and our deepest desires, and as we remain faithful, He, like a loving father, envisions the fun He will have in giving us our reward.

Even when it seems difficult, even when the task is hard, stay faithful. Right now, your Father is planning for the best monster hugs ever, with you as the giggling recipient.

Revolving Door

Come to me, all who are weary and burdened,
and I will give you rest.
MATTHEW 11:28

Aimee felt like her life was caught in a revolving door. Each day seemed like the day before, with no way out of the routine. She pulled herself out of bed each morning and headed to the kitchen to brew that necessary pick-me-up called coffee. After preparing lunches and cooking breakfast, she dropped the kids off at school and battled traffic on the way to work. It felt as though she had already done a days work.

Once she arrived at the office, she had telephone calls to return and a mountain of paperwork to tackle. Problems crowded out the pleasure her career was supposed to bring. Trapped in that revolving door, she just went around and around, doing the same things day after day.

Dinner was just as routine as the rest of her life. What will it be tonight? she wondered. *Chicken, pork, or beef. If it's Tuesday, then it must be beef.* Even the revolving schedule of food preparation kept her in the same rut. Exhaustion set in as she piled pots and pans into the sink after dinner. She had to find a better way of getting through the day! Aimee realized that the only thing she could change was her attitude.

The next morning when she woke, she prayed first, the first step out of that revolving door. She kissed and hugged her children, sang in the shower, dressed, and hurried to her car, slowing down for a moment to notice the flowers in bloom. When she got to the office, she thanked God for the opportunity to work for such a good company. The revolving door began slowing down. That night, she transformed the same old beef into beef stroganoff and the dishwashing into a family affair. The kids had never seen her this way, and they didn't want to miss a minute of it.

If your life is stuck in a revolving door, step out and enjoy the peace that God offers. He'll be with you all along the way as you pray, sing, and change your tune.

The Hand of Friendship

This is command: Love each other.
J O H N   1 5 : 1 7

I t's not always easy to love. Growing up, Ben and Mary constantly fought. As brother and sister, they were inseparable, but they were interested only in tormenting each other—a push here, a shove there, stolen cookies, disappearing toys.

One spring afternoon, their mother reached her limit. She sat down both her young children and looked from one to the other. "I've had enough of your fighting. For the rest of the day, I don't want to hear a single raised voice, a thud from hitting one another, a scream, or a cry. I want you to play nicely, love each other, and be kind. Period. End of story. Just do it." She got up, brushed herself off and went back to her tasks, unable to do or say anymore.

Ben and Mary sat and looked at each other. Love each other? How could they love each other? Just by being told? Especially when the sight of the other was enough to bring mud bombs and hair-pulling to mind? But they had never seen their mother quite so angry.

A few moments passed in silence, until Ben finally reached out and took Marys hand. "Want to build a fort?"

Mary smiled and said, "Okay."

Of course, it's not always quite as easy as grabbing someone's hand and playing soldier, but it's not as hard as we might think. Sometimes loving each other is simply a matter of letting go, starting anew with a fresh page before you, and deciding that the past is gone and that all you have is the future to mold. It's a matter of extending your hand in friendship and choosing to play rather than argue.

God commands us to love one another. Can you think of someone you have refused to love? Is there something you can do to extend a hand of friendship? Even if it is rejected, God asks only that you do your part. He will see to the rest. You never know; it may work out better than you imagine. They might even say, "Okay!"

Adopted for Life

For he chose us in him before the creation of the world to be holy and blameless in his sight. In love he predestined us to be adopted as his sons through Jesus Christ, in accordance with his pleasure and will.

E P H E S I A N S   1 : 4 - 5

Some years ago, Jack brought Susie home from a "foster home" because his wife wanted a basset hound. Instead of the beautiful tri-colored animal she expected, Susie was the color of red Georgia clay and something less than beautiful.

At first, Helen wanted to return the dog. It really didn't suit her tastes. Susie wasn't a show dog, she had no pedigree, and from what the woman could see, she wasn't even very special. After a week, however, she and the dog bonded.

Susie became a protective member of the family, barking at strangers and routinely following Helen's children to school. As the years passed, Susie developed quite a character. During a regional football playoff one year, Susie darted onto the field to retrieve the football. The referees had to stop the game and carry her to the sidelines.

One time, Helen received a desperate phone call from a boy in her old neighborhood. She could hear the pain in his voice as he said, "You need to come over right away. Susie's not moving." Fearing the worst, she and her older boys drove down the street.

Susie's still form was lying in the crabgrass. The woman leaned out the window and called, "Susie!" The animal didn't move. She opened the car door and walked slowly toward the motionless body. She saw one lazy ear perk up. "Thank goodness," she whispered, "she's still alive!"

Just as Helen leaned down to see how badly she was hurt, Susie jumped up and gave her the sloppiest dog kiss ever. Throwing her arms around the dog, she realized Susie was as much a part of her family as any of her children.

When we are adopted into the family of God, we are no longer a part of the world's family; we are part of a heavenly family that serves a sovereign Lord. What a blessing to be His child!

A Bubbly Challenge

*Sons are a heritage from the Lord, children a
reward from him.*
P S A L M   1 2 7 : 3

Sometimes, being a mother is simply not easy.
One dreary winter day, Barbara, the mother
of two toddlers, felt discouraged as she
swept up cookie crumbs and wiped up spilled juice.
She was exhausted from trying to prevent her two little
ones from getting into one thing after another.

While she answered the doorbell, her daughter
slipped into a white eyelet dress to parade around the
kitchen in bare feet. Barbara picked up her unhappy
child and marched her into the bedroom to change.

After putting shoes on the children, she planned a
trip to the store. Setting both of her toddlers in front of
the television for a moment, she went into her bedroom
to get ready Before she could zip her jeans, she heard
an earsplitting shriek from outside. She dashed out the

back door and caught her daughter innocently letting the cat out of the cooler.

"What was that cat doing in there?" she asked.

Before her daughter could answer, she heard her three-year-old son squalling. He was lying face down on the other side of a three-foot high brick wall. Through his tears, he said, "Sissy pushed me." Barbara half-believed Sissy had put the cat in the cooler so there'd be no witnesses.

After fussing at her children for their disobedience, the woman felt a tug at her angry heart. "Please, Lord," she prayed, "Give me peace and patience with my children."

Later that evening, as the kids were taking their evening bath, Barbara heard giggling and laughing, so she peeked in on her little "angels." To her dismay, the room was filled with bubbles. Not a bit of bubble bath was left. Then she discovered that her bottle of peach-scented shampoo — her favorite — was completely empty But the impatience she had felt earlier that day was replaced by a joyful, laughing heart.

Our ability to see our children as a blessing from God is sometimes a challenge. That's when we need to think as a child and discover how much fun is tucked away in a bottle of sweet-smelling shampoo.

Above the Clouds

"For my thoughts are not your thoughts,
neither are your ways my ways," declares the
Lord.
ISAIAH 55:8

Denise rested her flushed face against the cool window. It had been hours since she had left her warm bed to fight her way to the airport. Finally, she sat on the plane, which was preparing to taxi onto the runway.

This trip, unlike many others, brought none of the familiar pleasure to her heart as the plane began to move . . . no vacation . . . no friend's wedding. This trip was a somber one to visit her ailing father in a distant state.

Her father was sick; her husband was frustrated and angry as his company transitioned to a younger, more "able" staff; and her teenage son was pushing the envelope to fit in with a group of students Denise feared and disliked. Why was all of this taking place now? Why, Lord? She had prayed! She had always lived a life worthy of blessing and reward—or so she had thought.

As the plane slowly rose into the air, Denise surveyed the land below her. Dark and dreary under a cloudy, rainy sky, the entire landscape seemed to fit her mood. Slowly, the plane began to break through the clouds, and Denise could no longer see the land below. They seemed to be lost in a gray mist until they climbed on top of the clouds. What a difference! The dark, menacing clouds were transformed into soft white blankets, The blue sky and sunshine were bright and unwavering on the other side.

Does life seem dark and dreary from your perspective? Are you living beneath the dark clouds of depression or sadness? It's hard to see the light in the midst of the storm. But remember, just beyond the cloud cover is an amazing sight. Today, allow God to show you life from His perspective.

The God Factor

*For where your treasure is,
there your heart will be also.*
MATTHEW 6:21

Surrounded by stacks of invoices and receipts, Theresa's fingers flew over the number pad of her keyboard, recalculating and checking the year's expenditures and income. She couldn't believe how much money their employees had wasted on copy paper. Still, it looked like they were going to make a good profit for the first time this year. Thank God! she thought wearily. They had finally licked their turnover problem by providing better healthcare coverage and dental insurance.

Theresa picked up her coffee cup and walked down the hall to the small kitchen their company provided. One of her employees sat at the table reading her Bible and eating a microwave dinner.

"What are you doing here so late?" Theresa asked, pouring another cup of coffee.

"Oh, hi, Mrs. Chase," Angela said. "I thought I'd work tonight and get out that report you needed by tomorrow afternoon."

"You don't have to do that," Theresa said.

"I know, but I just wanted to double check my figures."

"I appreciate all your hard work."

"Thanks," Angela said, smiling and closing her Bible. "And thanks for letting us start a Bible study group in the morning. We've been praying for you and the business, too."

"It's working!" Theresa said. "Keep it up."

Instead of the conventional wisdom, which says that a business should only make decisions based on the bottom line, the relationship between an employer and an employee is a symbiotic one. It takes a cooperative effort to achieve success. Some companies finally are realizing that there is a "God factor" at work when a business cares sincerely for its employees and sows appreciation as well as benefits into their lives. If you are a business person, consider allowing your employees to start a Bible study or prayer group during lunchtime, or before or after work. Invite God into your workplace, and He will honor your trust in Him.

Seeds of Care

A new command I give you: Love one another.
As I have loved you, so you must love one
another.
JOHN 13:34

As Jennifer eased the batter-dipped, sliced green tomatoes into the frying pan, the aroma brought back vivid memories. The snapshots in her mind were sharp and clear as she remembered her mother marrying the man from Alabama. Jennifer had been a teenager from the city, and she couldn't stand this man from the "sticks." To her, he was nothing but a country bumpkin.

Early one spring morning, everything changed. She was sitting on the backyard swing, watching as he turned the soil with a shovel on a sunny spot behind the house. Each day, he did something different: he'd break up dirt clods, toss rocks out, and add compost, finally raking the soil smooth. Curious, Jennifer walked across the garden, feeling the coolness of the newly worked earth between her toes.

"Here," said her stepfather, "Take these." He poured some seeds into her open hand.

"What are they?" she asked, feeling her resentment dissipate in the cool morning.

"Squash," he said. "Later, I'll plant pole beans and tomatoes."

She watched that day as he planted the seeds, covering them with dirt and patting it down. Following his example, she soon completed a row of little mounds.

Later that summer, she enjoyed looking under the leaves of the squash plants and plucking the golden vegetables. She also liked the taste of a young cucumber, but most of all, she loved the green tomatoes her stepfather taught her to fry.

Jennifer smiled at the memory and at her eleven-year-old son, Jon, who waited patiently for the fried green tomatoes to cool. What her stepfather had done that day was to crumble the wall between them, much like he'd broken up the soil. Looking at her son, she knew that same love would continue for yet another generation.

Are you sowing seeds of love? Or are your seeds falling onto hard soil? Take the time to nurture and care for your "seeds." Break up the hard ground of resentment, and allow God to cause your love to grow in someone's heart.[5]

A Heart of Hospitality

When Priscilla and Aquila heard him, they
invited him to their home and explained to him
the way of God more adequately.
ACTS 18:26

Because of Jeff's profession, he and Rochelle relocated many times over the years. However, one of the relocations was memorable not because of something that happened, but rather because of something that *didn't* happen.

Jeff was required to begin his position in a new city before their home was ready for occupancy. A woman from a local church heard about his predicament and offered Jeff the use of her family's guest room until their home was ready.

When they finally moved into their new house, Rochelle wanted to show her gratitude to the woman for her kindness to Jeff. She called and asked her to stop by for tea, apologizing that she'd probably have to sit on a few packing boxes but assuring her that she would be most welcome. There was a slight pause before the woman replied, "No, dear. I won't come over just now. I'll wait until you have things the way you want them. Then we can have a nice visit."

The woman was no doubt only trying to give Rochelle some extra time to settle in. But things didn't quite work out the way she thought they would. Rochelle never seemed to get things "the way she wanted them." Some of the living room packing boxes stayed in the dining room for a few months, as they waited for repairs to be made to the living room floor. Then when those boxes were emptied, the dining room disintegrated into a mess of wallpaper, paint, and floor tile samples for the kitchen. By the time those things were taken care of, nine months had gone by, and Rochelle was too embarrassed to re-extend her invitation of hospitality.

A hospitable person is gracious, cordial, and generous. Hospitality asks us to open our hearts to others, whether our homes are picture perfect or not. And when we refuse hospitality, we may be hurting the heart of a stranger. Let's keep our hearts open to give and receive hospitality. We're sure to find God's blessings — and quite possibly a friend, too.

The God Who Never Sleeps

Cast all your anxiety on him because he cares for you.

1 PETER 5:7

In March of 1975, a tornado raked an eight- mile path across Atlanta, Georgia, snapping pine trees like so many toothpicks. Civil defense officials estimated the damage to be as high as thirty million dollars.

Even today, Gloria remembers that day as though it were yesterday. She was a younger woman then and had worked part-time as a secretary at a small office. The office was closed that Monday so employees could attend a memorial service for a co-worker.

That morning as Gloria got ready for the service, she noticed the skies outside turn an ominous black. The wind picked up, and trees bowed like rubber. She watched metal garbage cans being tossed down the street. Then the driving rain hit. The last thing on Gloria's mind, though, was a tornado.

After attending the service, she drove home. Visibility was poor as the rain slanted in sheets across the road. When she passed by her office, she almost wished she had gone to work, so she wouldn't have to battle the weather all the way home. The constant scraping of the windshield wipers grated on her nerves, so she turned on the radio to drown out the sound. The news reports were unbelievable! A tornado had been spotted in the Atlanta area. She accelerated, urging her car toward home.

Not until later did she learn that the tornadoes that whipped through Atlanta had destroyed the building where she worked. When she finally went back to the office and surveyed the damage, she found everything in a shambles. She trembled when she saw the collapsed concrete wall on top of her desk and shuddered to think what might have happened had she gone to work.

What a blessing to know that God is omnipresent! He is the One who neither slumbers nor sleeps. He promises to be with us and deliver us even in the midst of a whirlwind. Look to God when darkness blankets your world, and He will show you the way home!

Deliverance

From the Lord comes deliverance.
P S A L M   3 : 8

S ue watched the burning ember of her last cigarette glow in the dark. She was sitting out on her back step as close to the stroke of midnight as possible.

"Oh, Lord," she whispered in the quiet night. "Please let this be it! I can't take failure anymore. I can't take this addiction anymore. Please take it away from me, Lord. I beg You — deliver me!"

With a flourish of confidence, she crushed out the remaining ember and tossed it to the side. Staring into the darkness, she felt certain that this time she would succeed. This time was for good.

Out of the darkness came the sound of a small bird. Sue cocked her head and listened closely. It was odd to hear a bird chirping so late in the night. There, by the edge of the patio, was a cardinal. Sue watched in awe as the bird walked along the cement and turned its head to catch her eye. She had never seen one so close nor one so bold, and she somehow knew that God was assuring her of His presence.

The next day, when the headaches came, she reminded herself of the Deliverer. When the stress came that normally would have driven her to hide in her addiction, she lifted her head and remembered the cardinal. And when her addiction to nicotine subsided, she thanked God and felt His pleasure.

God has the power and the ability to deliver you. No matter how many times you think you have disappointed Him, He graciously reaches out and lifts you up again. Turn your life over to your Heavenly Father, and watch Him create something wonderful.

The Hand of God

*For he will command his angels concerning you
to guard you in all your ways.*
P S A L M   9 1 : 1 1

Charlie Shedd, author of more than thirty-five books, once told about a time when he felt God's touch. He believes angels have often made themselves known to him by a pressure, a touch, a warning, or an urging. According to Shedd, the Bible often uses "the hand of God" to reveal God's presence.

One evening as Charlie drove into his garage at suppertime, he turned off the automobile ignition but found that his fingers just wouldn't let go. "What's going on here?" he asked out loud.

An inner voice seemed to say, "Go see Roy." From the spot in his heart where he and God conversed, he knew the Holy Spirit was giving a command. Charlie argued, "But it's suppertime." And God's voice seemed to say, "Supper can wait, Charlie. Go."

Charlie's thoughts ran rampant, but he switched on the ignition and went. But why? he questioned. He'd just seen the senior citizen in church the day before, and he seemed fine. The only response to his question was silence.

Charlie drove to Roy's house less than a mile away, where he found Roy on the floor, calling for help. Roy had tripped over a stump, breaking his glasses and cutting his face. Charlie wondered how the elderly man made it home; he had injured himself six miles away.

Later, Roy thanked Charlie for coming, then asked, "How did you know I needed you?"

Charlie answered, "I think it was an angel, Roy." To which Roy promptly responded, "Makes sense. I was lying there on the floor, praying you'd come."

How many times have you heard the quiet voice of the Holy Spirit urging you to respond? How many times have you dismissed Him? Pray this day that God will open your heart to His whisperings and follow His leading to minister to others. If you listen, you will hear Him in the place where you and the Lord hold dialogue.[6]

Giving Thanks

Do not be anxious about anything, but in
everything, by prayer and petition, with
thanksgiving, present your requests to God.
PHILIPPIANS 4:6

The Thanksgiving table stood ready, a plump turkey in the center and a myriad of side dishes that seemed to cover every remaining square inch. The aroma of stuffing wafted from the oven door as Susan set out the deviled eggs.

The combined smells brought back the first Thanksgiving that Susan could remember. She had been a five-year-old then. That year she had contracted strep throat, which developed into rheumatic fever. She was sick for days. Her mother handled the sickness matter-of-factly, although she probably knew the risk of heart damage. Throughout the day and night, Susan would hear her mother slip into her room to check on her.

After the danger passed, Susan went to the doctor and learned that for the next year, she would not be allowed to run, exercise, or even walk fast, in order to prevent heart damage. That fall, as brightly colored leaves skittered to the ground, Susan walked slowly to school and back home again.

November arrived, and her kindergarten teacher prepared a Thanksgiving skit. Susan was excited as she dreamed of becoming one of the Indians who danced around the stage. But instead, she was told she would have to play the part of an oak tree. It was disappointing, but her mother taught her to be thankful anyway. At least she was part of the play.

Standing at the stove, Susan stirred the gravy. Other Thanksgivings came to mind—seasons when she'd lost loved ones. Although those were the hardest, she was thankful that God had blessed her with people who had made a difference in her life. And a smile graced her lips when she thought of the Thanksgivings when her children were toddlers. She could almost hear the kids sitting on the floor banging on pots and pans with wooden spoons.

Susan brought her mind back to the present as her family began arriving. Her grandchildren burst through the back door, and she hugged each one. And looking heavenward, she thanked God for all the memories yet to be made.

Destined to Win

Carry each other's burdens, and in this way you
will fulfill the law of Christ.
GALATIANS 6:2

Anne-Marie could feel the stitch in her side as she drew each ragged breath. Ten more strides, now five, now two. She held her arm out and handed the baton to the runner waiting in front of her. "Go, go, go!" she yelled. Her friend, Misha, took the baton and began to run. Her pace was quick and her prospects good, if only because she was refreshed and ready to run. Anne-Marie bent over and filled her lungs in great gasps. She could not have run another step. Thank goodness, Misha was ready.

That's what teamwork is all about. As lovers of God, we carry the weight of responsibility to be there for our friends. We hand off to one another the care and love of our Father. When one is weary, the other is strong; when one is disheartened, the other believes

That's the way God designed the system to work. We're not supposed to run our race alone!

Sheryl experienced this firsthand. After a bout of illness in her family, her church and small Bible study group had taken turns visiting and bringing her dinner. Now she had the opportunity to do the same as God blessed her with health and healing.

Like a well-trained, cross-country running team, we need to be refreshed and ready to run when the baton is handed our way. Yet we also need to be willing to receive when we can't walk on our own. Love and care for one another is the light by which we see our God. It's the best "warm fuzzy" in the world to know His love so intimately.

Is there someone you can love today? Someone who may need a card, a thought, a prayer? Or are you the one with the stitch in your side, ready to receive? In either case, allow yourself to reach out and be a part of the team that God has put together. We're destined to win!

Prayer for Harried Moms

He will take great delight in you, he will quiet you with his love, he will rejoice over you with singing.
ZEPHANIAH 3:17

F inancial hardship had forced Valerie to take a part-time job delivering newspapers. The route took two hours, and she had to bring her two young children along with her.

After sitting at the kitchen table stuffing papers in plastic bags, the family was ready to go. Valerie started out with her two toddlers, a box of crackers, two apples, building blocks, a purple dinosaur, extra diapers, and seven stacks of newspapers.

While she had gotten used to dodging large trucks, commercial buses, and a herd of goats, she could never quite get used to her daughter repeatedly asking, "Mom, what can I eat?"

"Eat an apple," Valerie answered.

From the back seat came the reply, "They're all gone." The distraction threw Valerie off, and she missed a mailbox. She backed up and stuffed a paper in.

"Then eat a cracker," she said, biting her lip. Turning around, Valerie saw half the box of crackers littering the back seat. She groaned and said, "Amy, hand me a newspaper."

Halfway through the paper route and in the middle of nowhere, Amy started whining. "What's wrong, sweetheart?" Valerie asked.

"I've got to go to the bathroom."

Valerie gritted her teeth and pleaded, "Hold it."

"I can't!" Amy wailed.

Valerie turned the car around and headed for the nearest fast-food restaurant, but it was too late, and she reluctantly headed home for a change of clothes. With only forty minutes left, Valerie and her helpers arrived back on the paper route. Just as she stuffed the last paper in a box, she heard a hissing sound and stopped the car. Looking at the flat tire, she cried, "Lord, are You there? I can't deal with one more thing. Please help me." Just about then, she heard singing coming from the back seat. "Jesus loves me, this I know . . ."

The Lord does love us. He loves us whether we're about to scream in exasperation or ready to shout for joy from a rooftop. When we know God is in ultimate control of everything, we can turn our circumstances over to Him and feel His love surround us like a beautiful symphony.

Unspoken Prayer

Do not be like them, for your Father knows what
you need before you ask him.
MATTHEW 6:8

The kitchen phone jarred Jody's thoughts. "I'll be there as soon as I can," she said, turning off the bubbling stew. Hurriedly, she hung up. "Come on, Tim," she called, "let's go pick up your sister." Her daughter would be waiting outside in thirty-degree weather following the school's choir rehearsal.

Both mother and son shivered as they pulled the car out of the driveway. The heater had finally begun to blow warm air as they rounded a corner and headed up a back street toward the school. Just ahead, under a street light, they spotted a small brown-and-white dog, lying motionless. The headlights lit up the dog as Jody slowly drove around the animal. Starting up the hill, she glanced in the rearview mirror.

"It moved," she said. "Son, that dog's alive!" She pulled the car over and jumped out, running back. Tears filled her eyes as she allowed the injured animal to smell her hand. "Go get help!" she shouted.

"There — at that house!"

Tim raced up to the nearest home and banged on the door. The man who answered, fearful of being bitten by the dog, refused to help and closed the door. When her son explained to her what had happened, she prayed silently about what to do next. Although her daughter was waiting in front of the school and was probably cold, she was torn by the idea of leaving the dog alone. It was so helpless.

Of the few cars that traveled that back street, none would stop. Then as if God had heard her unspoken prayer, a black sport utility vehicle drove up and out climbed a man wearing a green medical smock. After checking the injured dog, he said he'd be glad to take it in for treatment. It turned out that he worked for a local veterinarian in town!

On reflection, Jody knew she had felt the real presence of God on that back street late on a cold winter night when the exact person she and the dog needed appeared. How comforting to know the Lord hears our prayers and answers them even before we speak the words! God cares deeply for all His creatures — even injured dogs.

Walking Through the Pain

For he has delivered me from all my troubles.
PSALM 54:7

"Yes, you're going to the doctor's office," Jean said. "That's the only way you can be on the basketball team."

"But, Mom," whined Jamie. "I hate doctors! Maybe I'll just lay out of basketball this year." Her teenage daughter leaned back in the kitchen chair.

"Don't be silly," Jean said and motioned for her daughter to follow her to the car. "Basketball tryouts are in three weeks, and you have to take a physical." Jean slid behind the wheel of the car. "Now hurry up, or we'll be late." Dragging her feet, Jamie crawled into the car and fastened her seat belt.

"They won't hurt me, will they, Mom?" Jamie asked in a small voice.

"Of course not."

Inside the waiting room, Jamie fidgeted as she sat on the wooden stool waiting for the nurse. After what seemed like hours, the nurse first checked Jamie's height and weight and then requested that Jamie do a series of jumping jacks. Jamie grimaced at her mother and began jumping. The nurse checked her pulse rate. After Jamie's breathing returned to normal, the nurse asked, "Are you ready for the finger stick?"

With a look of betrayal, Jamie glared at her mother. "Will it hurt?"

"A little," the nurse said. She grasped Jamie's middle finger and quickly pricked it.

"That hurt!" Jamie hollered, examining the damage.

"You know," her mother said, trying to distract her daughter, "When I was pregnant, I had to have a finger stick every six weeks."

The teen's blue eyes twinkled, and a little smile played along her lips "You don't have to worry, Mom. The way I hate pain, I'm going to adopt."

Life is not always that easy. There isn't any way to prevent someone from experiencing pain, but learning about God's love is the best way to deal with life's ups and downs. God never promised that He would always protect us from pain and suffering, but He did say that He would walk with us through it and deliver us. Let God take your hand!

IN THE KITCHEN WITH GOD
IN THE KITCHEN WITH GOD

Big Brother

*Contend, O Lord, with those who contend with
me; fight against those who fight against me.*
P S A L M   3 5 : 1

———————————————

Tara looked at the big bully in front of her
and stuck out her tongue. She knew she was
taking life and limb in hand by being so
reckless, but at this point, she really didn't care. She
was tired of being pushed around, tired of being made
fun of, and tired of handing over her lunch money to a
boy who didn't appear to need another morsel of food
for the next fifteen years.

Plus, she had a backup plan, a card she had been
holding close to her chest—a card that would forever
relieve her of intimidation from this bully. As it
happened, today was the day to stand up and fight.

"You little . . ." The big boy took three menacing
steps in Tara's direction, then stopped in his tracks.
Looking over her left shoulder and then her right, the
bully began to tremble and slowly backed up. Tara

stood quietly as her three older brothers walked past her and continued to advance on the boy.

Her oldest brother, Peter, grabbed the boy's shirt and pulled him close. "This is your one warning — your only warning." He spoke slowly, dramatically. "Mess with our sister again, and we'll personally see to it that you never eat lunch again, or dinner, or breakfast . . . or anything. Understand?"

The boy nodded, refusing to look at Tara, then turned and ran.

God is our Protector. If we bring Him into the battles of daily life, there is no enemy that He cannot conquer with a simple word. He is better than a protective big brother. He is the ultimate knight who fights the battles we cannot fight on our own.

Maybe no one is stealing your lunch money, but perhaps you're allowing something or someone to steal your joy, your peace, and your passion for life. Allow the King of kings to step in and fight for you. He loves you and will never abandon you. He loves taking on the bad guys to bring lightness, peace, and confidence to your step. There is no bully alive that He cannot conquer.

The Rusty Nail

As *the Father has loved me, so have I loved you.*
JOHN 15:9

I n the corner of the kitchen, beside the huge oven, an old rusty nail protruded from the wall. It looked as if it had been there for many years. When Cecilia, a gray-haired grandmother, was not in the kitchen, her apron hung securely on that nail. Each time she entered her domain, she immediately reached for her tattered apron and tied it around her waist. It was worn and faded from years of use. Chocolate syrup stains and grease spots covered the huge pockets on the front.

She owned dozens of aprons. Some were made of solid colors, and others were covered with brightly colored designs. Many still had the store tags on them. All of them looked much better than the one that hung on the old rusty nail. When her granddaughter asked her why she preferred the old one to the others, she said that it was a special apron, since it was given to her with love. Cecilia never explained why it was so special, but the love it symbolized was evident.

Many years ago, old rusty nails held Jesus Christ on the cross. The need for a sacrifice was what placed Him there. His love for His children is what kept Him there. The King of kings was reduced to a battered man as a crown of thorns was placed on His head. And as the rusty nails were driven through His hands, He wept. He focused on His love for us and His ability to provide the ultimate sacrifice of love. He was worn, much like the old apron. Blood stains covered His body as He said, "It is finished (John 19:30)."

On the third day, the stains were washed away, as Jesus Christ rose bodily from the grave. The scars that were created by the old rusty nails remain visible in the palms of His hands. Those scars represent a kind of love that man can't fully understand, but Gods love is obvious, as He holds all His children close to His heart.

Sweet Tooth

The little foxes are ruining the vineyards. Catch
them, for the grapes are all in blossom.
SONG OF SOLOMON 2:15 TLB

Eleven-year-old Gracie opened the refrigerator door, enjoying the cold draft of air after her walk home from the bus stop. She took a long swig of water from the pitcher, then headed straight for the cookie jar. Her sweet tooth demanded to be satisfied! Unfortunately, the cookie jar was empty. Before Sissy had left for college, it had always been full of Grade's favorites: peanut butter. Of course, that was in 1960 before anyone had ever heard of good and bad cholesterol.

Gracie had watched her older sister make peanut-butter cookies hundreds of times. Why couldn't she do it herself? She didn't even need a cookbook. With a determined spirit, Gracie gathered all the ingredients for her first baking attempt—butter, vanilla, sugar, eggs, baking soda, peanut-butter—and creamed the mixture together. She tasted the dough. It was almost as good as Sissy's. But something was missing. Flour!

Gracie opened the flour canister, but it was empty, too. Maybe she could substitute something. Gracie peered into every cabinet, stretching up on her tiptoes, until she spotted a brown paper bag with a dusting of flour on the outside. She scrambled up on the kitchen counter, retrieved the sack from the top shelf, and looked inside. Flour! It was all she needed. Gracie eagerly stirred in the flour to make a stiff dough and dropped the mixture by spoonfuls onto the cookie sheet. Then she used a fork to make the crisscrosses on top and popped the pan into the oven. She could hardly wait!

When the cookies were golden brown, she removed them from the oven and set them aside to cool. But she couldn't wait; she gingerly picked up a hot cookie and tossed it back and forth in her hands, blowing on the surface. Her mouth was actually watering as she tasted her first bite.

"Yuck!" she exclaimed. It was salty! Gracie spit the cookie out in the sink just as her mother came in and discovered her daughter had used the coating mixture for frying chicken.

Sometimes a small substitution might not seem important, but the wrong ingredient can ruin the whole recipe. It's the same way in our walk with God. Little white lies might not seem that important, until they spoil the day.

———————————————

Hidden Beauty

O Lord, our Lord, how majestic is your name in
all the earth!
P S A L M   8 : 9

Shortly after the New Year arrived, Brenda noticed the clutter on her dining-room table. She thought of the Christmas celebration just a few weeks earlier and how beautiful her table had been as she welcomed church members into her home. Just being with her friends made the evening special.

Now life was back to normal. The tree was packed up, and the nativity scene had been put away. The elegant setting had been removed from her table and replaced with several bills that needed to be paid. Contributing to the jumble was a box of tissues (the remnant of a bout of pneumonia that had slowed her pace during the holidays) and an address book.

Brenda picked up the address book and flipped through the pages. Each page was filled with names, addresses, and telephone numbers. She realized that this book represented her family and friends, and she thought about how fortunate she was to have so many people who loved her. As she read the names, she offered up a prayer for each one. She prayed for their special needs and asked God to walk with them daily.

She picked up the tissues and thanked God for her health. Then she looked over the bills and thanked God for her career and the opportunity to provide for her family. One by one, she counted her many blessings.

At first glance, the things on Brenda's table seemed to invade the beauty of her home, but as she looked at each item, she realized that each one served as a reminder of God's presence in her life.

The Kingdom Family

Whoever does the will of my Father in heaven is
my brother and sister and mother.
MATTHEW 12:50

Charlene walked down the aisle on her fiancé's arm. This had been the moment she was supposed to share with her father, the precious time when he would give his blessing to her marriage and officially hand her over, as she made the transition from daughter to wife.

Yet her father was not there. Nor was her mother or sister. Her family had a previous commitment, a convention they had to attend, and that convention had been more important than her wedding. It had been a tough blow, and Charlene could feel the pain clouding this special moment.

There, waiting at the altar, was her pastor—her shepherd. His warm and tender smile received them into his presence. Charlene felt her longing subside as she looked into his kind face. The pastor and his wife had been better than family. They had counseled, laughed, and cried with Charlene as she worked through premarital jitters. They had prayed with her and held her hand. They were more father and mother to her than her biological parents had ever been.

Charlene smiled from the depths of her heart at her waiting bridegroom. This was a time to celebrate the new, and God had been faithful in surrounding her with parents, brothers, and sisters that were part of His kingdom.

Have you lost your family? God is faithful in providing people who will nurture us, love us, and fill the empty spaces in our lives. Your family doesn't have to come from the same womb or share the same blood. Allow Him to give you the gift of His family. We are meant to be that for each other.

Light and Fluffy

What shall I compare the kingdom of God to? It is like yeast that a woman took and mixed into a large amount of flour until it worked all through the dough.

LUKE 13:20-21

"What's that, Grandma?" the little girl asked, as she watched her grandmother carefully mix the ingredients for bread.

"Yeast," Grandma replied. "That's what makes the bread rise. We have to cover the dough with a cloth and put it in a warm place if we want our rolls to be light and fluffy."

Not fully understanding the way yeast works, Mary was impatient. She continued to lift the cloth in order to see the round balls of dough that sat in the baking dish. After a while, she realized that they were growing larger.

Finally, Grandma placed the rolls in the preheated oven. Mary watched through the glass window as the tops began turning golden brown. The scent permeated the whole house. When the rolls were done, Mary was allowed to brush a small amount of butter on the top of each one.

Mary's grandmother thought about the look of amazement on her granddaughter's face when she saw how the bread had doubled in size. Her faith, she realized, was a lot like that dough. The more she prayed and studied Gods Word, the larger her faith grew. And just as the rolls needed to remain warm in order to rise, she needed to keep her heart warm in order to serve God and others.

Today, keep a warm smile on your lips and a glow in your eyes. With a "light and fluffy" attitude toward life, we can rise up in the midst of trouble and show others the warmth that only God can provide.

———————————————————

Mama's Kitchen

A cheerful look brings joy to the heart, and good news gives health to the bones.

PROVERBS 15:30

"Ma, how about whipping up some of those hoecakes?" Pa had shouted many times through the years.

Ma always knew what those words meant. Pa was hungry. She never failed to put down what she was doing to go to the kitchen to prepare something for him to eat. She was a remarkable woman who could turn even the smallest amount of food into a delightful meal. Once she tied her apron around her waist, she was transformed into the best cook in the world.

As she stirred up the cornbread mixture, she hummed old-time gospel hymns. The hot, black, iron skillet sizzled when she dropped spoonfuls of the mixture on the pan. Somehow those hoecakes were always perfectly round and browned just right. Ma always said that the secret was in the pan. But the real reason for her success with cornbread was the cheerful presence of God in her heart.

After the hoecakes were cooked and dinner placed on the table, Ma always thanked God for the food. And once the blessing was offered, she would start to hum those old tunes again. While the hoecakes filled Pa's stomach, Ma warmed his soul with love.

God always blesses those who depend on Him. Ma offered a little; God gave a lot. She taught by example that the way a person lives reveals much more about that person than what they say. Ma was a shining example. We can all learn from Ma and the many "grandmothers" in the faith who have gone on before us. When we rely fully on God, even the simplest tasks make life richer.

Closing the Door

*We want each of you to show this same diligence
to the very end, in order to make your hope sure.*
HEBREWS 6:11

M ichelle looked around her office and felt a sigh rise from the depths of her soul. She had worked so hard for all of this and had put so many hours into her vision, especially at the beginning, when her company had only been a dream and her energy was committed to making the dream come true. Someone else had appreciated her creativity — a bigger, larger company that had bought her out in a forceful merger. Now all that was once hers belonged to an unseen face. It was like losing a family member.

Michelle looked out of her office window at her employees. She knew they had been looking to her, waiting to see how she would handle herself over the past four weeks. She was tempted to throw all her energy into a new pursuit, but she also knew that she had a commitment to see this old one to its end. It was a matter of integrity. The new company would never know if she spent her time—their time now—on this new pursuit. But she would know, and her employees would know. That's not how she wanted to do business. With a forced smile, she sat at her desk and focused her mind on the issues of the day. When she finally handed this company over, she would do so knowing that she had done her best to the very end.

Change takes place in all of our lives. One season ends, and another begins. We may say goodbye to a job, a relationship, a town, or a dream. With each ending, we have a choice. We can walk away without looking back, ignoring the closure and attention that's needed, or we can take the time, painful as it may be, to finish well—to tie up loose ends, to say our goodbyes, to work hard right to the end, and to give of ourselves freely so we can begin a new adventure, knowing we have closed out the old one with integrity.

Is there an area of your life that needs attention today? Something that needs to be finished well? Take a moment and ask God to help you close the door. Only then will you be blessed in your new beginning.

The First New Shoes

The King will reply, "I tell you the truth,
whatever you did for one of the least of these
brothers of mine, you did for me."
MATTHEW 25:40

A s the Depression continued, the kitchen cabinets remained empty. Money was scarce. Their father couldn't handle the pressure and left again. As the oldest son, Jerry hit the road to try to earn some money to buy food for his three younger brothers. The air was bitterly cold, and the ground was frozen.

As Jerry walked, he saw some men digging a hole beside the road. "Can I help?" he asked.

"Sure," one of the men said as he handed him a shovel.

Jerry worked hard. For hours he dug in the bitter cold through frozen dirt until sleet pelted the ground. The men handed him a few coins before quitting. The young boy stopped by the corner market to buy some canned goods for Christmas dinner the following day.

As he walked out of the store, the rain and sleet picked up and poured down harder upon him. He had placed cardboard inside his shoes to replace the worn-out soles, and that had worked fine until the cold water soaked his socks and feet. He sat down on the cold ground to adjust the cardboard.

"Son, are those the only shoes you have?" a man in uniform asked.

"Yes sir," Jerry replied.

"Come with me," the man said and took him to a shoe store down the street, where he bought Jerry his first ever pair of brand-new shoes.

The light of Christmas shone brightly at the kitchen table as Jerry's family enjoyed the meal that he had earned the day before, digging a ditch in the freezing cold. The love of Jesus—and the memory of a kind man in a uniform—brought tears to Jerry's eyes as he thanked God for taking care of them all, even in the worst of times.

Kitchen Cat-astrophe

Look at the birds of the air; they do not sow or
reap or store away in barns, and yet your
heavenly Father feeds them. Are you not much
more valuable than they?
MATTHEW 6:26

Cindy put down her glass of iced tea and reached for a cookie. "How are we going to pay all these bills?" she asked in exasperation. "And what about the kids' school clothes?"

Tim chewed on the pencil eraser a moment, then took a swallow of tea. "I don't know," he said, "but you've got to quit hounding me and let me think. There's got to be a way."

A scratching noise at the back door caught Cindy's attention. "What is that noise?" she asked, getting up to check on it. As she opened the door, the family's black-and-white cat raced in. "He's got something in his mouth."

Cindy screamed when the creature wiggled. The cat, taken aback by all the fuss, dropped the bird he was holding between his teeth. And free once more, the bird soared to the kitchen window right above the kitchen sink and perched on a curtain rod, looking quite content.

"Do something!" Cindy shouted. Tim raced into the bathroom for a large towel. He eased toward the bird, startling it in the process. Again, the bird was on the wing. Cindy ducked as the fluttering wings nearly caught in the strands of her hair.

"We need to calm down," she said. "We can't do anything while we're this anxious." She took a deep breath and retrieved the towel from her husband. In one quick swoop she threw the towel over the unsuspecting bird. Gently, she carried the creature to the back door and turned it loose.

She marveled at the lesson God unfolded before her. "Look at the birds of the air, honey," she said, "are we not more valuable than they are? Doesn't God say He will provide for us?"

God has promised in His Word to be our provider and supply us with all our daily needs. In His eyes, we are more precious than the birds that dominate the air.

The Key Ingredient

*This is the day the Lord has made; let us rejoice
and be glad in it*
P S A L M   1 1 8 : 2 4

"He's coming home, honey!" Caroline shouted to her husband.

Their son, Brad, had left home for college a few months earlier, leaving their home much too quiet and empty. The phone hardly ever rang, and the doorbell remained silent. His absence took a toll on Caroline's emotions, causing her to retreat from the things that she always enjoyed.

Now he was coming to visit. Excitedly, Caroline changed the sheets on Brad's cold bed, remembering the many nights she knelt beside him as he said his bedtime prayers. For the last few months, she had wished so many times that she could kiss him goodnight before retiring for the evening. After she fluffed his pillow and straightened up his bedroom, she breezed into the kitchen to bake his favorite dessert — a buttermilk pound cake.

All the ingredients were on hand, and she almost had the recipe memorized. She measured them out carefully and made every effort to mix it as directed, but before all the flour was mixed in, the phone rang. After a brief conversation, she returned to the cake. She poured the batter into the baking pans and hurriedly placed them in the preheated oven.

About halfway through the baking time, she looked into the mixing bowl. Oh, no! She had left out a large portion of the flour! A quick glance into the oven confirmed her fears; the cake was not rising. She was so disappointed. Despite her good intentions, she had left out most of an important ingredient. The cake might taste okay, but it was flat and gooey.

Life is a lot like that cake. Some experiences may seem to be good and offer happiness, but without Christ, the most important element of life is missing. Do you have all the ingredients for a fulfilled life?

God is in Charge

The righteous cry out, and the Lord hears them;
he delivers them form all their troubles.

P S A L M   3 4 : 1 7

Linda stood at her kitchen counter, peeling potatoes. None of her adult children could manage to get away to visit on Father's Day. She fumed as she cut up potatoes and dropped them into a pan.

When a friend had given her husband, Hank, two tickets to a Braves game, she had been elated. "Surely one of the kids can go with you," she had said. She called one son, but his wife was working that day, and he had to stay with the children. Their second son lived in another state, and son number three had other plans. She had not been able to reach their oldest son.

When Sunday arrived, they had just about decided to give the tickets to someone else when Doug, their oldest son, called to wish his dad a happy Father's Day.

His dad explained the predicament, having tickets to the game and nobody to go with. Immediately, their son said, "I can make it. Since we're running short on time, why don't you just meet me at the stadium?"

There was a flurry of indefinite directions, and then Hank was off to the game. Ten minutes later, their son called and anxiously asked, "Has Dad left yet?"

"Yes, about ten minutes ago," Linda said. "Why?"

"My keys are locked in the front seat along with my wallet,"

Promising to relay the message if her husband called, Linda hung up. "Lord," she prayed, "Please be in control of this situation. Help Doug find his father."

Four hours passed before she heard from her son. "Did you make it to the game? Did you find him?"

"Actually," her son said, a ring of laughter in his voice, "I picked him up on a street corner. He looked like a lost and deserted dad. And yes, we made it to the game . . . and the Braves won. What a great day!"

When one thing after another seems to go wrong in our lives, it's good to know we have a Father in Heaven who cares about even the smallest, most intimate details of our lives.

The Storms of Life

*And we know that in all things God works for
the good of those who love him, who have been
called according to his purpose.*
R O M A N S   8 : 2 8

One cold winter day in the 1960s, a major ice storm hit central Georgia. Power outages were rampant throughout the area. Some people owned fireplaces or gas heaters, but others who were less fortunate were forced to seek shelter in the homes of their neighbors.

One particular family didn't have any source of heat except for the gas stove in their kitchen. For days, while they huddled together around the kitchen table, the heat from the oven kept them warm.

They could cook, while some of their hapless neighbors could not. Many nearby residents brought over cans of soup to heat on their stovetop. Hospitality intensified as a bitter cold spell set in.

Sitting around that table and the glow of a single candle, the family laughed and shared stories and events that were important to each of them. They hadn't done that in months! While the television was out of order, they put their lives back into place. As a result of that storm, the family grew closer. Each one of them remembered the light from that candle for years afterwards.

Sometimes we don't realize what's missing in our lives until we cease all of our busyness. Spending quality family time together is important to God. But you don't need to wait for an ice storm or some other crisis to draw your family close.

God is always faithful to show goodness in every situation. Just as the glow of the candle provided light during the storm, He lights our way through the darkest and most difficult days of our lives.

Help!

And let us not get tired of doing what is right,
for after a while we will reap a harvest of blessing
if we don't get discouraged and give up.
GALATIANS 6:9 TLB

What was I thinking! Kristy stood in the middle of the church's commercial kitchen and turned around slowly. As the hubbub from the fellowship hall continued, the dirty dishes were piling up on every possible surface.

"I've already loaded the dishwasher once," her friend, Carol, said, "You can wash pots and pans until the cycle is finished. I'm sorry I have to desert you, but I really have to run."

Kristy felt overwhelmed, but she didn't want to complain. "No problem . . . really."

By the time dishes were washed, dried, and put away, she and another woman were the only ones left in the kitchen. Mrs. Carson, an elderly woman who had been in their church forever, had taken pity on her and stayed to help.

"I don't know what I would have done if you hadn't stayed," Kristy said, smiling. She hugged her plump helper.

"Oh, this was nothing, dear!" Mrs. Carson said. "You should have been here before we had a dishwasher."

"I can't imagine."

"Of course, people were a little different back then. We all pitched in, and the work was done in no time. Now people are so busy; they're stretched to the limit. I suppose even you have to get up and go to work in the morning."

"Yes, ma'am."

"Well, you might not get many thank-you's from other people, but God sees your heart. He's pleased with you. Now let's get you home."

When you feel like no one else cares about doing what's right or pitching in to help, remember, God cares, and He will extend His grace to you.

Think on These Things

*Finally, brothers, whatever is true, whatever is
noble, whatever is right, whatever is pure,
whatever is lovely, whatever is admirable
— if anything is excellent or praiseworthy —
think about such things.*
PHILIPPIANS 4:8

Irene Harrell, author or co-author of more than two dozen books, once wrote about an argument she had with one of her teenage sons before he slammed out of the back door. She recalled clenching her fists and gritting her teeth in anger. The teen had spared no expense in irritating his mother, and she was ready for a verbal fight. But the boy was saved by the bell—the telephone. By the time Irene had finished the call, her son was nowhere in sight.

Later that day as Irene went about her household chores, she complained to her younger son, James, about her older son's transgressions. After finishing a load of dishes, she found her young son deep in thought.

"I think I know what would help you with Tommy," James said. Not knowing what to do with her teenager, she listened carefully to her son's advice.

"Just don't think about it," he said matter-of-factly.

While she swept the kitchen floor, this childlike suggestion rolled around in her mind. Then she turned her thoughts to God, concentrating on His grace and mercy.

Later, when her teenage son came home, she was able to treat him with the same mercy. Instead of an angry mother, Tommy found grace as Irene offered him an ice-cream float before he went to bed. She was surprised to find her son, who'd been braced for a scolding, responding in love. To her great surprise, the boy washed his glass and spoon that evening and mumbled, "Thanks, Mom," as he shuffled off to bed. The next morning, a change had come over her son. Irene found Tommy lying in bed, smiling, and actually doing his homework.

Is there someone who needs your forgiveness? Today, think on these things—whatever is noble, right, pure, lovely, or admirable![7]

Joy in the Morning

*Weeping may remain for a night, but rejoicing
comes in the morning.*
P S A L M   3 0 : 5

"Guess what I've got!" Grace shouted. Her two sons raced in to see what was in the box.

"It's a kitty," whispered four-year-old Donnie. A smile played around his mouth. Hesitantly, he reached inside and stroked the orange tabby's head. "What's his name?"

"He kind of reminds me of a ball of sunshine," his mother said. "Why don't we call him Sunny?" Recently divorced, Grace hoped the new kitten would help the boys get over their loneliness for their father.

"Let's feed the kitty," she said as she opened a can of cat food. The whirring of the can opener excited Sunny, and he climbed up her pants leg. Gently, she pulled the kitten from her, setting him in front of his food. Donnie and his brother watched the kitten eat every mouthful.

But as evening shadows crossed the room, Grace felt depression stalking her again. How would she ever raise her sons without any help? The divorce had not been easy, and the emotional battering had taken its toll. Later that night, she lay in bed, still battling the sadness.

The next morning, Donnie crawled into bed with her and the kitten. With sunlight streaming through slatted blinds, they cuddled and watched Sunny swat at dust balls. It was easy to smile at the kittens antics, but she wondered if she would ever be happy again.

Donnie picked up the kitten and put him on his lap. Gently, the boy patted its head, then rubbed the kitten behind its ears. Soon the cat began to purr — loudly. Donnie leaned down and listened, his eyes widening in surprise. "Mom, my kitty's swallowed a motorcycle!" he said. Grace burst into laughter, rejoicing that God had given her such wonderful children.

Sometimes, we all sink into a well of discouragement. When that happens, thank God for the small things of life, even when you're walking in the valley of shadows. Let Him turn your weeping into joy.

The Tattered Bible

Let the word of Christ dwell in you richly as you teach and admonish one another with all wisdom.

COLOSSIANS 3:16

S arah's worn and tattered cookbook sat on a desk in the corner of the kitchen. Some of its pages were stuck together with drops of cake batter or cookie dough. Practically every page was stained, but it was obvious which recipes were her favorites. Those pages were barely readable. Between the leaves of the book were recipes from newspapers and store packages that she had carefully cut out over the years.

Sarah couldn't get along in the kitchen without her trusted cookbook. Not only did it provide a list of ingredients needed and instructions for preparing her favorite dishes, it provided many useful facts to enable her to run her kitchen efficiently.

"Learning to read a recipe correctly is the most important part of cooking," she told her daughter many times.

Sitting close beside that trusted cookbook was the Bible. Like the cookbook, its pages were worn. It held clippings of memorable events that had taken place in her life and the lives of her family members over the years. Ink spots dotted the pages of her favorite Scripture passages. After many years of use, certain verses were difficult to read.

"Learning to understand the Bible and using it as a guideline for life is the most important part of living," she told her daughter. "This is Gods instruction book designed especially for us. Everything that you will ever need to know about life is written on these pages."

By her example, Sarah taught her daughter that a used Bible is the most valuable tool for living. She sought Gods guidance through His Word on a regular basis. Not only had it provided her with security and hope, it also helped her to live a life pleasing to Him.

That tattered Bible explained a lot about Sarah's life. All the ingredients and instructions were there; she only needed to follow them in order to find the strength, wisdom, and courage that characterized her life.

Pass it On

In truth I perceive that God shows no partiality.
A C T S   1 0 : 3 4   N K J V

Through the years, kitchens have played a major role in Connie's life. When she was growing up, she lived on a farm surrounded by aunts, uncles, cousins, siblings, her mother, and her grandmother. She often remembered the hot summer days when the kitchen would be steamy because they were canning. Canning was a family affair. The men raised and harvested the crops; the children peeled, chopped, and prepared the produce, and the women cooked and did the actual canning. There was much lively discussion over recipes, techniques, and timing.

At some point during the day, Grandma would sneak Connie under the table and give her a taste of whatever was being canned. (She especially liked Grandma's pickled peaches.) Grandma would warn her to keep this their special secret. In fact, it was such a secret that Connie didn't find out until a few years ago that Grandma did this for all her cousins and siblings. That discovery didn't make them love Grandma any less. It made them all feel special.

Because of it, Connie always thought she was Grandma's favorite grandchild, and that knowledge has sustained her through many rough times. When she found out that everyone in her generation thought they were Grandma's favorite grandchild, it didn't diminish that special feeling. Connie didn't feel betrayed. She was awed by the love that Grandma gave to the whole family. Her grandmother became the model for the kind of person she wanted to be.

God is the same way. He loves each one of us as if we were the only person in the universe. We are individually and personally His own special children.

Now as Connie makes gingerbread men with her own grandchildren, she passes along to them the knowledge that each and every one of them is as special to her as they are to God and prays that they will someday pass it along to their own grandchildren — maybe even in the kitchen.

———————————

Saturday Morning Bagels

He will call upon me, and I will answer him; I
will be with him in trouble; I will deliver him
and honor him.

PSALM 91:15

When the kids were at home, Saturday mornings were always filled with cartoons, good-natured teasing, and cereal spills on the carpet. Now that they had the house to themselves, Nancy and Garth preferred to go out for breakfast. Cereal and toast had been replaced by warm, cinnamon-raisin bagels, hazelnut-lite cream cheese, and cappuccino.

At first, their empty nest had been lonely, but after a period of adjustment, the couple had learned to talk about other things besides the children. Their favorite breakfast spot played classical music, and they always sat in the high stools near the window, leisurely reading the morning paper and planning their day together. They were more in love now than they could have even imagined when they were first starting out.But that's not how it had always been. Their love had deepened and matured, as they grew in their own relationships with Christ.

If your marriage seems rocky right now, don't give up on it just yet. God has a plan for your lives together. When you think you're going to break under the stress of kids and bills and in-laws, send up a prayer (or several) tor help to get you through the day.

Marriage isn't simple, and it isn't always chocolate and roses. Sometimes it's getting up for a glass of cold water in the middle of the night when your spouse has a sore throat. Other times it might be holding a light as he works on your broken-down car in a chilly garage, or saying, "I'm sorry," first when you've hurt her feelings.

God hasn't promised in His Word that you will never experience difficulties. But He has promised to deliver you out of them all. Be encouraged!

Kitchen Friends

A man who has friends must himself be friendly.
PROVERBS 18:24 NKJV

---

*H*ow wonderful to see the goodness of God in my own kitchen, Jennifer thought as she browsed through her cookbook collection. He had provided abundantly for her and her family. Not only did they enjoy a variety of good foods, He had provided the kitchen and all its tools. He also had given her a talent she loved, cooking, and it was not just for herself but for the enjoyment of her family and friends. And God had given her the joy of discovery. Jennifer loved finding new ideas and recipes. While reading about food, she had discovered that the "old" nutritional values found in the book of Leviticus in the Bible are just as valid today as when God gave them to the Israelites when they came out of Egypt.

People loved to visit together around her kitchen table, probably because her yellow kitchen was bright and cheerful. They seemed to feel warm and accepted there. Over the years, her table had been the scene of a lot of sharing, delight, heartbreak, good times, games, food, and plenty of fellowship. On holidays, everyone trooped in and out of the kitchen, helping with the cooking, visiting, carrying cups of coffee or other drinks to family members, stirring, laughing, and bumping into each other.

One day, Jennifer saw a holiday commercial on television in which the woman was thankful for instant food so she could get out of the kitchen and spend more time with her family. She wondered why the woman's family didn't spend more time in the kitchen with her!

Even the family who is not in Jennifer's kitchen at the moment is still participating in what is going on. She remembered one year when her mother was making gravy at the stove while her dad, who was sitting in the living room, kept calling instructions to her and answering her questions as to amounts of ingredients and stirring time.

Is your kitchen the kind of place where everyone feels comfortable and welcome? If not, how can you make it a spot that binds you closer to your family and friends and to God? It might be as easy as planning a pizza night or baking chocolate chip cookies together. Give it a try!

Coming Home

No eye has seen, no ear has heard, no mind has conceived what God has prepared for those who love him.

1 CORINTHIANS 2:9

A manda trudged through the snow on the Connecticut hillside. It had been a great afternoon of sledding, playing, and snowballs. She had thrown the perfect snowball at her teenage son, Cody. He'd grinned and looked at her through snow-covered eyelashes. "Nice shot, Mom! But look out! I'll get you back!" Amanda had attempted to run but didn't get far before her mischievous son had helped her land face- first in the soft snow.

Now they made their way back on the seemingly endless snow-covered path. By the time Amanda opened the front door to their home, she could barely feel her nose, her ears, or her fingertips. "We're back!"

she called to her mother, who was busy making hot chocolate in the kitchen.

Amanda and the children peeled off their frozen layers and settled into the warmth of the living room couches. Grandmother bustled in with cups of steaming hot cocoa, and the smell from the kitchen indicated warm cookies were on the way. Amanda curled her fingers around the heated cup and smiled at the rosy cheeks of her offspring. There was nothing like it! Nothing eclipsed the feelings of home, of warmth, of coming in from the cold to the waiting hot chocolate.

God is preparing us. He watches from the window as we make our way across the cold and barren landscape. The minute we walk through the door of Heaven, we will be overwhelmed with the love of a gracious, waiting Father. It will be a celebration of peace, of coming home—the feelings of pleasure and joy more intense than we can even imagine. No matter where you are today, no matter what pain or what joy you are experiencing, it is nothing compared to the pleasure we will know in the light of God's presence . . . a cup of hot cocoa after a cold winters day . . . that kind of love . . . that kind of homecoming.

The Real Stuff

O Lord, you have searched me and you know me.
P S A L M   1 3 9 : 1

Veronica placed the cake on the dining room table. Wiping the sweat from her brow, she surveyed the scene before her. Streamers lined the ceiling, cups and plates were set out, and the warm glow of candles added the perfect touch. It was her Henry's seventieth birthday; Veronica was determined that it be an extra special occasion.

The guests began arriving, and Veronica directed them to the living room. It didn't work. It never seemed to work. Every time she had a gathering, people always seemed to gravitate toward the kitchen. Veronica sighed as she pushed through the crowd to finish her preparations. Everyone was laughing, talking, and seemed right at home. Veronica stopped for a moment as a friend warmly embraced her. She couldn't stay angry

The kitchen was the heartbeat of her home. It didn't matter what room she intended for people to go to, they always ended up in the kitchen, gathered around the table like family. Veronica smiled. The mess didn't matter; the fancy decorations in the other rooms didn't matter. It was the heart that people wanted—the real stuff—the comfort of home.

God is the same way in His love for us. He doesn't need the fancy stuff. He doesn't require hanging out with us at our formal best. He loves who we are—the messy, comfortable heartbeat of our very beings. That's the people He wants to spend time with, the ones He's drawn to, the ones He created. You don't have to fake.

———————————————

Future Father

And whoever welcome a little child like this in
my name welcomes me.
MATTHEW 18:5

June surveyed the crowd before her. The noise seemed too much, almost overwhelming as everyone tried to speak at once. It was Sunday dinner and all the family was gathered around the large table. Steaming platters of food were being handed from person to person as plates were piled higher and higher with delectable treats.

Down near the end of the table sat Daniel, a friend of June's youngest child, Nate. Daniel was only eight years old and looked flustered and nervous as people passed food around and over him. June watched as one of the other children noticed, and attended to him. "Would you like some of these potatoes, Daniel?"

The small boy nodded and smiled a simple grin of appreciation. The others seemed to take notice of him then and began asking him questions about school and friends. June knew that Daniel had a difficult home life. She was proud of her children as they focused on his hopes and dreams and seemed genuinely interested. "What do you want to be when you grow up?" asked one of the children.

Daniel hesitated and looked around at the family.

"I want to be a Dad. With lots of kids, like this family."

The room got quiet as everyone mulled over what he had said. Finally Bob, the oldest, smiled broadly and patted Daniel on the back. "Sounds great, Daniel! You'll make a great father!" he said, winking, "as long as you have a better group than this one to work with!"

The room exploded as all the kids laughed and began shouting over each other, yelling their defense. June watched Daniel in the rising commotion. He was sitting quietly with a smile on his face. Finally he grabbed his fork and seemed to nod to himself as he ate his first big bite. He seemed . . . triumphant.

Is there a little one you can love on today? Someone in your home, your church, or your neighborhood? Just a few small words of encouragement, a pair of listening ears, an afternoon in the midst of your family, can make a difference in the life of a child.

A Loaf of Bread

Love your neighbor as yourself.
LEVITICUS 19:18

Janice looked at the recipe book and then back to the mixing bowl. She kept up a constant stream of conversation with herself as she added each ingredient. "Okay . . . okay, Janice. One egg, one cup of flour, one banana . . . mix well. Don't mess this up, just take it slow. How hard can this be? Not hard, not hard at all! They'll love it!" She paused. "What if they don't love it? What if they think I'm a horrid cook, out to poison the neighborhood?" She shook the thoughts away, determined to press on.

Later that evening, Janice wrapped her slightly misshapen loaves of banana bread in plastic wrap. After a deep breath, she walked to her neighbor's home and rang the doorbell. An older man answered and greeted her in surprise. "Hi."

"Oh, hi! Yes . . . um . . . I'm your neighbor, Janice. I wanted to bring you this loaf of banana bread." Her cheeks reddened. "Well, basically, because I thought you might like it . . . not that I'm a great cook or anything. I mean, it IS actually edible, it's just that I'm not exactly what you would call a professional."

His grin interrupted her. "Really?" He reached out a tentative hand and took a loaf. "That was so very kind of you. I love banana bread."

Janice wanted to grab it back. He loved it? Oh, no! What if it was terrible? What if she turned him away from fruit breads for life?

He seemed to read her frantic thoughts. "I'm sure it's wonderful, Janice. Thank you. You made my evening . . . just with your thoughtfulness."

Janice smiled, relieved.

It's risky to give of ourselves! Sometimes we hardly know how to share friendship and love with our neighbors. What we do, though, isn't really important. It's the thought, the time, the interest we show that makes a difference in those around us. Take a moment and think of the neighbors on either side of your home. What can you do this very day to let them know you care?

References

Endnotes

[1] *Masterpieces of Religious Verse,* edited by James Dalton Morrison. (New York: Harper & Brothers Publishers, 1948).

[2] Nanette Thorsen-Snipes. Adapted from *Power for Living,* April 1992.

[3] *Brush of an Angel's Wings,* by Charlie W Shedd. (Ann Arbor, MI: Servant Publications, 1994).

[4] *Ordinary Days with an Extraordinary God,* by Irene Harrell. (1971).

[5] *After the Storm: Learning to Abide,* Nanette Thorsen-Snipes. (Star Books, 1990).

[6] *Paul Harvey's The Rest of the Story,* by Paul Aurandt. (New York: Doubleday & Company, 1977).

[7] Ginger Galloway. Adapted from *Guideposts,* August 1997.

Additional copies of this book and other titles in the *Quiet Moments with God* series are available from your local bookstore.

Breakfast with God
Coffee Break with God
Daybreak with God
In the Garden with God
Sunset with God
Tea Time with God
Through the Night with God
Christmas With God

www.ingramcontent.com/pod-product-compliance
Lightning Source LLC
Chambersburg PA
CBHW061153120626
46546CB00005B/2045